Satan Unmasked

SATAN UNMASKED

overcoming the Jezebel spirit

Colin Dye

Dovewell Publications

Dovewell Publications
Kensington Temple
Kensington Park Road
London
W11 3BY
England

Scriptural quotations are from the New King James Version, Thomas Nelson Inc., 1991.

ISBN 1-898444-01-3

Produced and printed by Gazelle Creative Productions Ltd,
Concorde House, Grenville Place, Mill Hill, London, NW7 3SA

CONTENTS

1.	the force of evil	9
2.	behind the mask	29
3.	Satan on the attack	77
4.	Jezebel exposed	125
5.	the way of victory	151
6.	confess and forsake	181

For this purpose the Son of God was manifested, that He might destroy the works of the devil.

1 John 3:8

1

the force of evil

MANY PEOPLE IN WESTERN EUROPE and North America do not believe in a devil and demons. They think that the discoveries of the contemporary 'scientific' age somehow make it impossible for an intelligent person to accept that evil spirits really exist.

They mock the popular idea of an impish figure with horns, hooves and tail, and suggest that this cartoon-like character is what the Bible teaches about Satan.

But the Scriptures do not describe the devil and his demons in this simplistic way. Instead, they warn people about a malign force of evil which is behind all the sinful structures and events of the world, and behind all the tempting pressures that are endured by every man, woman and child.

However, even though many unbelieving western people may now reject the idea of a 'devil', they still often identify a particular event or person as being 'evil' or as being influenced by 'evil'.

Terrible events like a terrorist bomb exploding in a crowded café, or a mass murderer killing for pleasure, or a power-crazy tyrant torturing opponents, cause even the most hardened unbeliever to recognise that a great force of evil must somehow exist.

It does. And the Bible calls the leader of this force 'Satan' or 'the devil'.

THE LAST ONE HUNDRED YEARS have produced a terrible list of names and events which bear instant and powerful testimony to the sickening effects of the malign force of evil which is at work in our world.

The Somme, Verdun, Josef Stalin, Adolf Hitler, Pol Pot, Idi Amin, Fascism, Communism, Apartheid, Genocide, Ethnic Cleansing, the Ku Klux Klan, Pearl Harbour, Auschwitz, Hiroshima, Nagasaki, Chernobyl, Bhopal, Lockerbie, and so on.

These are only some of the many names which are international bywords for evil. Every country has its own national list of nightmares too, its own catalogue of events and people whose names chill the marrow - like, in Britain for example, Dr Crippin, Fred West, Dunblane, Hungerford, Dr Harold Shipman and the murder of James Bulger.

Whenever unbelievers try to explain how these people can possibly have acted as they have, they almost always have to fall back on the word 'evil'.

It is as though, deep in their innermost beings, they know that the participants in these events must have been influenced by a malignant, destructive force of evil – by something which is outside and apart from humanity, but which seeks to rule the world and to ravage its inhabitants.

EVEN THOUGH MOST PEOPLE RECOGNISE that a force of evil can influence others, they find it hard to admit that it may effect them.

The truth, however, is that every man, woman and child in the world experiences temptation. But only a wise few go on to realise that this has to point to the existence of a tempter.

Every human being, from the highest to the lowest, the brightest to the dullest, the oldest to the youngest, feels a pressure to do what they know to be wrong or to not do what they know to be right. There is nothing that you can do, nowhere that you can go, to escape from the tempting evil pressure to do wrong.

Of course, this pressure can sometimes be explained by human desires and social influences. But these are rarely sufficient to explain the sheer force of the universal phenomenon of human temptation.

If you've ever tried to break a bad habit which was formed by giving in to temptation, you'll have found that you're gripped by a force which is stronger than you, by a force which is determined to try and make you do what you don't want to do.

People give this force many different names, but the Bible calls it 'the devil' and his 'demons'.

CHRISTIAN BELIEVERS WHO ARE DETERMINED to do God's will, and who are grounded in God's Word, face an extra puzzling dilemma. It is one which can be adequately explained only by the existence of a malign force of evil which is actively and terribly opposed to God's people.

Most practising Christians know that God wants them to be 'fruitful' - both individually and collectively in the church. Yet they also know that most believers and congregations are nowhere near as fruitful as God intends them to be.

Perhaps you've read Jesus' words about the importance of bearing fruit 'one hundredfold', and you long for this to be your personal experience. If so, you've probably already found that there's something which is trying to prevent you from getting beyond the 'one fold' and 'two fold' level.

Deep down, you really want to do God's will, to speak God's words, to do God's deeds, to bring great glory to His wonderful name.

But, at times, it all seems so terribly hard. Sometimes when you start moving in God's will, it's as though you're walking in treacle, with lead weights on your shoes and a gag in your mouth.

Why is this? It's simple. It's because there's a great force of evil which is trying to stop you praying, to snatch your joy, to silence your witness, and to side-track you from God's good purposes.

Despite all your good intentions, and your genuine commitment to God, you've probably found that you're faced with an assortment of spiritual struggles which haven't got any easier with the passing of time.

You thought that the Christian life would get easier as you matured in the faith, but - instead - you've found that it has got much harder!

Why is this? The only explanation for these persistent struggles - which every believer endures - is that there is a tangible force of evil which is deeply opposed to God's purposes and God's people. This force - led by Satan, the devil, - is always doing its utmost to steer you away from God, from God's will, and from His peace and love and grace.

FROM THE DAYS OF THE NEW TESTAMENT, many Christian believers have noticed that they struggle particularly strongly with three great temptations – with sex, with money and with power. (You might have heard preachers refer to these as 'the girls, the gold and the glory'.)

Some of the most experienced and gifted church leaders, who have spent long years teaching people about the saving death of Christ, and helping them to 'live in victory' and be 'dead to sin', have eventually succumbed to one of these temptations.

The malign force of evil has had thousands of years of practise at getting through the defences of men and women who love God. The devil and his demons have honed their skills so well that they now know all your human weaknesses and vulnerable points, and are vastly experienced at persuading believers that the pleasures of sex, money or power are preferable to God's perfect path of purity, simplicity and service.

Indeed, Satan has such a strong grip on the world that you live in a society which accepts the devil's false ideas about sex, money and power, and promotes them as good and acceptable.

Even though it's hard to ignore the massive evidence of lives, homes, families and children all wrecked by giving in to sexual temptation, increasing numbers of believers are falling for the lie that 'it won't happen to them' and are foolishly accepting the fleeting pleasures of the flesh which are promoted by the force of evil.

It's the same with money and power. Even though Jesus' teaching about 'mammon' and 'servanthood' are stamped through the Gospels, more and more believers are heeding the devil's materialistic call for 'more' and are modelling themselves on Satan's tyrannical style of leadership.

The devil doesn't mind whether you're ensnared by sex, by money or by power. He just wants to ensnare you, to paralyse you spiritually, to strip you of your joy, to make you fruitless and miserable, to turn you into an ineffective believer.

If he can't get you through sex, he'll try to get you through money. If he can't get you through money, he'll try to get you through power, and so on. With several thousand years' experience in human temptation, he knows that these are your weak spots - and his demons home in on them ruthlessly.

YOU PROBABLY KNOW that the devil was decisively defeated at the cross, but that he will not be totally destroyed until the final day of judgement. You live in the time between his defeat and his destruction, and there are two equal and opposite attitudes which suit him very nicely.

First, he's delighted when people are preoccupied with him, when they blame him for everything, see him everywhere, talk about him continuously, and act as though his decisive defeat on the cross had never taken place.

Second, the devil is thrilled when people are sceptical about his existence and assume that he has no power at all. If the devil does exist, and his aim is to rebel against God and to involve the whole world in his rebellion, little could please him more than the way he is dismissed and ridiculed today!

The more that Satan can do to encourage people to doubt his existence, the better it is for him. In fact, you can say that the doubt about his existence is a big sign of his activity.

Satan is especially pleased when Christian believers don't take him seriously - when they aren't involved in the ministry of deliverance, and won't speak about the devil and his demons in front of their unbelieving friends.

After all, if more believers knew the real truth about Satan, he would surely be more hated, more resisted and more defeated.

That is the purpose of this book - to strip away the mask of Satan so that you see him as he is, so that you understand his strategies, hate him with God's righteous passion, resist him in Jesus' precious name, and overcome him in your life and family.

SATAN REJOICES WHEN PEOPLE IGNORE HIM, when they ridicule him and dismiss him as a figure appropriate for medieval myths but not for the modern twenty-first century. This leaves him free to operate in the world with the maximum ease and efficiency, confident that few will take him seriously.

Because of this, it's important that you're able to explain to people why Christians believe that the devil and his demons exist. But remember, we don't believe in cartoon figures with horns and tails.

Instead, we're sure that they're a force which is utterly ghastly, totally wicked, and completely opposed to humanity.

We're convinced that they're the malign force of evil which stands behind all other types of evil - physical, corporate, moral and spiritual.

We're certain that Satan is real, and that he is the unified centre and focus of all evil, and of all his demonic accomplices and underlings.

There are several good reasons for believing that the devil exists, and you should try to grasp them so that you can begin to refute the widespread scepticism about Satan in the society around you.

THE FORCE OF EVIL

THERE IS NO POWER WITHOUT PERSONALITY in our world. Of course, there can be a manifestation of power without an obvious personality, but the personality is always there in the background if you look deeply enough.

Quite simply, there cannot be power without an originating intelligence - planning, establishing and using it.

We live our lives with the assumption that we possess reason and free will, and that people interact through their use of reason and free will.

Christians believe that it makes little sense to reject the Supreme Reason in the name of reason, and then to accept rationality on the basis of randomness!

Instead, we conclude that a supreme intelligence, a supreme Reason and Will, lies behind everything we see in the world that is good - we call this God.

Furthermore, when we see the different forms of evil in the world, we also conclude that there must be an intelligent, originating spirit of evil behind all that is evil – and we call this Satan.

The marks of design in the world, the moral qualities of beauty, truth and goodness, all point to a good God. So too, the marks of design in the force of evil - which you hear about everyday – and the existence of the opposite of beauty, truth and goodness, all point to an evil originating personality that the Bible calls the devil.

In fact, without the devil, it would be difficult to conclude from all the wickedness in the world that God was a loving Father.

Believers who are sceptical about Satan need to ask themselves how they can balance God's goodness and the world's horrors. Without the devil, they are faced with a God who made the world as it is today, who created people as they are now, and who wills all the evil that takes place.

NOT ALL WESTERN PEOPLE ARE SCEPTICAL about the devil. A few worship him personally. And, over the last forty years, there has been a considerable growth in the whole area of 'the occult'.

More and more people have started to seek occult powers, to contact evil spirits, to try to talk to the dead, to learn about the dark forces, to become involved with the whole area of the spirit world without any reference to Christ.

When men and women deliberately seek occult powers, they soon discover that these things are real.

Others become involved more casually, through things like tarot cards, ouija boards, seances, horoscopes and levitation - and are often surprised by the reality of what they encounter and experience.

Of course, their experiences do not prove that a personal devil exists, but they do show that there is an invisible, concentrated power of evil which can affect people.

Outside Western Europe and North America, few people question the reality and power of the devil.

In Africa and South America, for example, even the most educated men and women are aware of the devil. Religions like Islam and Hinduism recognise that humanity has a great and terrible enemy. And hundreds of millions of ordinary people live in fear of the demons that they dread and try to placate.

Many western people dismiss the experience of other nations too lightly, but they cannot ignore the reality of their personal experience of temptation.

As you've seen, even the most sophisticated and educated Westerner feels the tug of temptation – and you need to encourage people gently to recognise the tempting force behind their tempting thoughts.

Everyone who tries to overcome their weaknesses, bad habits and failings soon discovers that they're surrounded by a subtle, cunning and persistent force. This common human experience should be enough to help you show people that Satan is a reality.

YOU SHOULD USE the biblical teaching about Satan to help sceptical believers appreciate his demonic reality.

Satan is a major Bible character. He appears from Genesis to Revelation as the great anti–God force of evil. He is in the Garden of Eden at the beginning of the story; he is at the cross confronting Christ; and he is in the lake of fire at the end of time.

In the Old Testament, Satan tempts Eve, Job, David, Saul, Joshua and the Israelites. He comes upon people, possesses them, and drives them to act against the will of God.

He is especially prominent in the four Gospels. In fact, there is more about Satan in these books than in the rest of the Scriptures, for the appearance of Christ drove the devil into a frenzy of desperate activity.

Throughout the rest of the New Testament, Satan is clearly presented as the tempter of men and women and the accuser of the brethren. He is shown to be powerful, but not all–powerful - a serious force who must be reckoned with by every believer.

The Scriptures teach that a personalised force of evil exists, and they name this force as Satan or the devil. This is not a small idea which is tucked away in a few half verses here and there. It is a prominent theme which runs through the whole Bible.

THE MOST IMPORTANT REASON for accepting that Satan exists is that Jesus clearly believed in him.

Jesus tells you more about Satan than anyone else in the Bible, and He never doubted his reality.

Satan opposed Jesus from his birth and repeatedly sought to destroy Him. He tempted Jesus in the wilderness, and kept on coming back to Him with devilish suggestions throughout His ministry. He snatched the message of the good news away from those who listened to Jesus half–heartedly, and sowed tares in the field of wheat.

Jesus taught His followers to ask their Heavenly Father every day to deliver them from the evil one. And He likened Satan to a strong man protecting his possessions until an even stronger man comes and casts him out.

Although Jesus knew that He was this stronger man, He knew that it would take the cross to defeat Satan. Jesus had to wrestle with Satan to the bitter end, without compromising one bit or weakening His resolve for one moment.

Jesus knew that the way of the cross would mean defeat for the devil. When He thought about the cross in John 12:31-32, He said, 'Now is the judgement of this world; now the ruler of this world will be cast out. And I, if I am lifted up from the earth, will draw all peoples to Myself.'

And, on the night before His death, Jesus said, in John 14:30, 'The ruler of this world is coming, and he has nothing in Me. But that the world may know that I love the Father, and as the Father gave Me commandment, so I do. Arise, let us go from here.'

With these words, the last great battle was joined - a life and death struggle in which nothing short of total obedience to the Father would suffice for victory.

The Gospels make it plain that Jesus had no doubts about the existence of Satan. For Jesus, the devil was His personal, powerful foe. For Jesus, there was no question about it, the devil was real, he was totally opposed to good, to God and to God's people, and he had be defeated – even at terrible personal cost.

SEVERAL MONTHS BEFORE THIS BOOK was written, I realised that I was feeling increasingly hedged in on every side of my life. It was as if there was some sort of spirit of confinement over me.

When I reflected on the previous years, I knew that I had enjoyed God's blessing in most areas of my life.

My ministry had matured and been blessed, and had taken me all over the world with tremendous fruit. The church I led, one of the largest in Britain, was growing. My marriage was strong. I was financially encouraged. But I knew that something was missing.

The fruit, in practically every area of my life, was less than I expected and less than I was sure God intended. In fact, it was not in proportion to the time, effort, and sheer commitment that I was giving.

The truth is that I was in danger of becoming seriously discouraged. I was having to fight feelings of wanting to quit, of wanting to release long-held but unfulfilled visions. I was confused, frustrated and heading for burn out. So I set myself aside for several weeks of prayer and fasting.

I was seeking the Lord for Himself in this time apart. Although I was thinking about some ministry issues, and had several matters of intercessory importance, my major focus was the Lord. It was during this time of seeking Him when God began to speak to me about Satan.

The Lord dramatically opened my eyes to the nature of the devil, and showed me how he'd taken hold of me – and was subtly tightening his grip to prevent me from fulfilling God's total plan for my life.

Finally, God said that He was going to help me see my authority over the devil, and start to use me to bring His deliverance to many people.

In particular, God showed me that the way the forces of Satan had worked through Queen Jezebel in the days of the prophet Elijah was extremely significant to our situation today.

God pressed me to expose the way that a 'Jezebel spirit' was working in-and-against the lives of believers today, and to help believers to start to resist this 'Jezebel spirit' in their lives and their churches.

When I returned to ministry after the time of prayer and fasting, the first thing I did was organise three nights of ministry at church about 'the Jezebel spirit'.

Without any exaggeration or over-statement, these were the most remarkable, powerful and liberating meetings of my entire ministry.

God stripped the mask of Satan away, and enabled people to see his malign personality and purposes. They began to hate Satan for what he had done and was doing to their lives.

They began to understand his diabolical strategies, to resist him in Jesus' name, to experience personal release, and to start to see him defeated in their lives and families.

This book has been shaped from the seminar notes I produced for these three amazing meetings, from the tapes of those meetings, from people's responses to the meetings, and from my further thoughts and study about Christ's triumphant victory over the force of evil.

THE DEVIL EXISTS. There's no doubt about it; he's real and he hates you. He wants to stop you in your tracks. He wants to destroy your marriage, your family, your ministry, even your very life.

He wants to neutralise you and make you totally ineffective in the spiritual battle you face. If you long to make a difference in the world for God, you can be sure that you're on course for a confrontation with the forces of Satan.

If you're on fire for God, if you want to be dangerous to the devil - to win souls, to live a holy life, to overthrow his evil works, and so on - he will throw his worst at you. His evil underlings will tempt you with sex, with money, with power, with whatever it takes to make you stumble.

But, when the devil does his worst, God does His best.

The time is short. The closer the Day of the Lord approaches, the more furious and desperate the devil's measures. Sooner or later, every 'on fire' believer will meet the 'Jezebel spirit'. And you must be ready to overcome it.

This book will help to prepare you for that meeting, and to triumph when it occurs.

2

behind the mask

GOD HAS GIVEN YOU HIS WORD, the Bible, to draw you to Himself, to introduce you to a living personal relationship with Christ, to fill you with hope, and to lead you along the path of everlasting life.

God's Word pays as little attention as it can to God's enemy, Satan, so it doesn't offer you a detailed description of the devil, his forces or his work. Instead, it merely provides you with all you need to know to resist the devil and his strategies.

Remember, you're called to resist the devil, not to define him; you're called to renounce him, not to describe him; you're called to trample on him, not to inspect him too closely.

We're not unmasking Satan in this book so that you can know him better, we're unmasking him so that you can overcome him in every area of your life.

Even so, it's natural to wonder how something as evil as the devil could have emerged in the perfect creation that God made. There are only three possible answers.

First, some people insist that the devil is merely a myth which was included in the Scriptures to explain the presence of evil - rather than a menacing reality who actually causes the evil. You've seen in the previous section that this is not the biblical answer.

Second, others maintain that the devil has always existed - and this is what most religions believe. They teach that there are two equal and opposite forces in the universe: one headed by God and the other by Satan.

This, however, is not the biblical teaching. The Scriptures declare that there is only one eternal and infinite being, and that even disease, death, sin and the devil are under God's ultimate control.

The third possibility is that the devil was created by God, that he was an important spirit of great ability who somehow became filled with pride and ambition, who rebelled, lost his position, and then set himself up on earth in opposition and hatred to God.

This is a rough outline of the biblical understanding. Satan is one of God's created spirits, for everything has sprung into being from God. You can see this in a passage like Isaiah 45:6-7, but it is especially clear in the book of Job.

According to the Bible, nothing happens in creation without the permissive will of God. He allows even what He does not will - confident that the final pattern will be beautiful. Satan, though powerful, is limited by his status as a created spirit: this means that he is ultimately subject to God's final authority.

THE BIBLE DOES NOT TELL THE FULL STORY of how this great created spirit fell, but it does offer a few important insights.

In Luke 10:18, for example, Jesus exclaims, 'I saw Satan fall like lightning from heaven'. Jesus had sent seventy of His disciples ahead of Him to announce the kingdom of God in words and deeds, and they had just returned triumphantly – with the news that even demons were subject to them in His name.

It's not clear what Jesus meant by these words. Perhaps He was looking back to a great cosmic battle at the dawn of time; or looking forward to Satan's final defeat at the end of time; or seeing a preview of the church's mission; or even something of all these.

What Jesus' words do show, however, is that Satan's original home was in heaven with God, and that he fell from this high position.

These words also remind you that there is a violent war on, and that God's people have power in Jesus' name over the enemy. Never forget this!

THE SECOND INSIGHT into Satan's origin comes in Revelation 12:7-9. In a prophetic passage about believers being persecuted in the Last Days, the apostle John writes:

'War broke out in heaven: Michael and his angels fought against the dragon; and the dragon and his angels fought, but they did not prevail, nor was a place found for them in heaven any longer.

'So the great dragon was cast out, that serpent of old, called the devil and Satan, who deceives the whole world; he was cast to the earth, and his angels were cast out with him.'

John was writing mainly to encourage you when you face persecution, but his words also shed light on Satan's origin. Once again, you see that Satan originally inhabited heaven, that he rebelled and was forcibly ejected – along with many other spiritual beings who had sided with him against God.

More importantly, the apostle John reveals that Satan's sphere of operations is now the earth, and that his main activity is opposing Christian believers in every possible way.

Be aware; behind your discouragement, depression and difficulties, behind your lethargy, fruitlessness and obstacles, behind every congregational division and evangelistic disappointment, there lurks a shadowy figure and his sinister accomplices who are intent on damaging you and crippling the church.

THE PROPHET EZEKIEL provides another glimpse into Satan's origin. The first ten verses of Ezekiel 28 describe the human ruler of Tyre and contain a prophetic message for him.

(Tyre was an island kingdom north–west of Israel which belonged to the Phoenicians. It was one of the most prosperous, powerful and proud kingdoms of that time. Jezebel was a princess of Tyre.)

The tone of the chapter, however, changes from verse 11 onwards. Ezekiel no longer refers to the prince of Tyre, but now to the king of Tyre. His words in verses 1–10 may be appropriate for a human ruler, but not his words in verses 12 and 13.

Surely these words can be applied only to Satan himself: 'You were the seal of perfection, full of wisdom and perfect in beauty. You were in Eden, the garden of God...'

Ezekiel's prophecy suggests that, after his creation, Satan was intimate with God. He lived on the holy mountain of God. He was blameless in all his ways, splendid in wisdom, skilful in operation and perfect in beauty.

Verse 15 states, 'You were perfect in your ways from the day you were created till iniquity was found in you'.

What was this iniquity? Ezekiel reports that 'the king of Tyre' was filled with violence through the abundance of his trading, that he became proud because of his beauty, and that he was corrupted by his knowledge.

Do you see some of the problems which caused Satan to fall? He became preoccupied with his personal beauty and with acquiring more and more knowledge for his own purposes and fame.

These are exactly the ploys that Satan used in the earthly kingdom of Tyre, that dominated the life of Jezebel, that characterise the enemy forces in Revelation 18, and that he still uses successfully to neutralise Christian believers.

Perhaps he's even tempting you with one of these ploys at the moment – if so, you'll know to ignore him now.

ISAIAH 14 OFFERS the other biblical insight into Satan's origin. Again, the first part of the chapter is a prophetic message to a human king – this time, the king of Babylon. But, from verse 10 onwards, a more sinister figure can be discerned behind the earthly king.

Surely these words can have been written only about Satan: 'Your pomp is brought down to Sheol and the sound of your stringed instruments; the maggot is spread under you and worms cover you.

'How you are fallen from heaven, O Lucifer, son of the morning! How you are cut down to the ground, you who weakened the nations.'

How did this creature come to fall? What did he do that was so terrible? What was the deed that first tainted perfection? What was the evil which laid the foundation for all future evil?

Isaiah 14:13–14 unveils the sin. 'You have said in your heart, "I will ascend into heaven, I will exalt my throne above the stars of God; I will also sit on the mount of the congregation, on the farthest sides of the north; I will ascend above the heights of the clouds, I will be like the Most High".'

Five times Satan said, 'I will', and this fivefold declaration of ambition and independence was the mother and father of all evil.

Satan was dissatisfied with his seat below God. He was not content to be number two in the heavenly hierarchy. He wanted to become God, to rule his own life, to receive public acclaim, to rule over others, to be number one in his world.

And so the devil tried to depose God.

This is why Satan fell. And the cause of his fall is his principal weapon in the war of attrition that he's waged ever since against God and His people – and that he's waging right now against you.

Most believers focus on denouncing the terrible effects of evil – on its damage and destruction. But, if you're to be an effective warrior on the side of good, you also need to focus on the essence of evil.

It's the two little words, 'I will'. It's thinking or acting independently of God's will. It's when someone assumes that they're number one in their life.

It's when you want to get your own way, to do your own thing, to be your own boss, to make your own decisions without any reference to the Lord. It's replacing the rule of God with the rule of self.

Satan's fivefold declaration of independence was the main reason why he was ejected from heaven, and this independent attitude is always at the root of every sin, every evil and every temptation.

As a result of the evil promptings in this area by Satan's forces, men and women have been giving way to pride, ambition and independent thinking from the Garden of Eden right to the present day

It's good that you should shake your head with sadness when another believer stumbles through the attractions of sex, money or power; but please also recognise the sinister essence which is beneath the superficial form of their sin.

Although fornication, adultery, seduction and homosexuality may seem rather different from greed, materialism, a lack of generosity, a lust for position and power, and so on, their essence is exactly the same.

It's thinking, 'I want this, so I will do this'; it's ignoring God's will and usurping His role and rule; it's deciding for yourself what you want without any reference to Him.

This independent essence is what is so terrible, rather than just the actual form of the sinful deed or thought.

Self–centred independent thoughts and independent actions are the exact opposite of the total dependence on God, and the intimate relationship with Him, that all God's creation was made to enjoy.

Even Satan was created to live in perfect companionship and harmony with God. He was made wise and beautiful; he was created as an 'anointed cherub' who had an important role in God's kingdom; but all this ruined when he started to think and act independently of God.

The iniquity of Satan's selfish ambition caused him to lose his ministry and to be expelled from the perfection of heaven. Then, when he fell, he took a great host of other spirits with him – and more people are still joining his rebellion of independence today. Make sure that you have nothing to do with him!

IT'S IMPORTANT YOU NOTICE that these insights into Satan's origin and fall are set in the context of a prophetic confrontation with the forces of darkness.

The apostle John refers to Satan's fall while he is describing the end–times struggle between the forces of evil and the church of God.

The prophet Ezekiel describes Satan's origin while he is speaking a strong word of the Lord's judgement to the human leader of Israel's enemy Tyre.

The prophet Isaiah gives his account of Satan's fall in the midst of a proverb against the king of Israel's enemy Babylon.

And Jesus, the anointed one, announces Satan's fall in the context of the proclamation of God's kingdom in words and mighty deeds by seventy of His disciples.

You've already seen that the four Gospels mention Satan more often than any other part of the Bible – because the appearance of God's anointed Son drove the devil into a frenzy of violent activity.

The context of these insights points to the same fact. Whenever God's people speak God's words in the power of God's Spirit, the devil and his forces always leap into action against them.

When, under the anointing of the Holy Spirit, you start to minister prophetically to someone who is held captive by the enemy, you're bound to arouse the devil's fury!

Satan's demons won't slink away quietly and release their captive without even a whimper. Instead, they'll mark you out for special attention. They'll target you with cunning temptations. They'll focus their wrath on your loved ones and family.

They'll do their utmost to persuade you to think or act independently of God, to trip you through the attractions of sex, money or power, to neutralise you through pride or ambition – so that you don't bother them again.

Don't despair! For, when the devil does his worst, God always does His best!

THIS PROPHETIC CONFRONTATION with the forces of evil is especially apparent in the story of Elijah and Jezebel.

Elijah the Tishbite was one of the mightiest prophets of the Old Testament, and he ministered in Israel during the reign of Queen Jezebel and King Ahab – whom the Bible describes as more wicked than all the evil kings before him.

God called Elijah prophetically to declare His name, to speak against the evil reign of Jezebel and Ahab, and to call God's people away from the worship of Baal and back to the worship of the true and living God. This didn't please the devil's forces!

1 Kings 16:31–34 describes the three great sins that Ahab committed against God and His people. First, he continued in the sins of King Jereboam, who had established his own order of priests and had mixed the worship of the Lord with the worship of pagan gods.

Second, Ahab married Jezebel, a pagan princess of Tyre who introduced her own false prophets and vigorously promoted the worship of Baal in Israel.

And third, he allowed Jericho to be rebuilt in direct disobedience to the revealed word of God.

Ahab's worst sin was his alliance with Jezebel. She soon took control of him and the whole of Israel. Jezebel is one of the clearest biblical examples of someone who is deeply influenced by Satan, and her name has become a byword for seduction, manipulation and tyrannical, violent power.

Nobody likes being called a Jezebel! Even the evil spirit in the shadows behind Jezebel can't stand being called 'the Jezebel spirit'!

Just as Ezekiel addressed an evil being who was behind the human prince of Tyre, and as Isaiah denounced the spiritual ruler behind the human king of Babylon, and as the book of Daniel refers to spiritual 'princes' of Persia and Greece, so too there was a spirit behind Jezebel who was opposed to God's people.

Like the 'kings' of Tyre and Babylon, the 'spirit of Jezebel' is one of those evil spirits who fell from heaven because of the devil's ruthless ambition to have his own way.

Under the influence of 'the Jezebel spirit', the Queen destroyed every visible trace of the worship of the Lord in Israel and killed as many true prophets of God as she could find.

The prophet Elijah was called and anointed by God to deal with this. In the power of the Spirit, he confronted the false gods and false prophets of his day, called the people back to God, and broke Jezebel's hold on the nation.

1 Kings 18 tells the story of God's victory through Elijah on Mount Carmel. First, he repaired the altar of the Lord; next, he called down fire from heaven; and then the whole nation cried out in repentance.

What a mighty victory! What a defeat for the enemy! And what a hornet's nest of trouble he stirred up for himself! Elijah's prophetic activity aroused the anger of 'the Jezebel spirit', and he had to face the full force of its wrath.

Anointed, prophetic words and deeds are a serious threat to the devil's forces, and they always respond with fury. It was so for Elijah. It was so for Jesus and the early church. And it is so for you too.

ALTHOUGH THE BIBLE sometimes speaks directly about Satan or the devil, it also refers to him more obliquely – like the sinister, shadowy figure behind the prince of Tyre and the king of Babylon. Satan is happy to lurk in the background as it often means that he can work more effectively.

Because of this, the Bible uses a large number of names, titles and descriptions for the malign force of evil that it calls Satan. It's possible to become a little confused by all the names, and to think that they each refer to a different spiritual being. But, although the scriptural names may be different, the underlying devilish characteristics are always the same.

You must realise that Satan is like a masked warrior, and that he uses whatever disguise is most likely to deceive his target.

Sometimes he'll appear to you as a roaring lion, and will try to scare you into submission. At other times he'll come to you as a devious serpent, and will try to deceive you into following his path. And many times he'll come to you as an angel of light, and will attempt to charm you into one of his snares.

Once you've learned to recognise Satan's superficially attractive masks, you'll be able to strip them from him and face him down – in Jesus' mighty name.

SATAN IS A HEBREW WORD which means 'adversary'. It's rendered in Greek by diabolos, which means 'accuser' or 'slanderer' and is usually translated into English as 'the devil'.

The Bible calls the force of evil 'Satan' and 'the devil' because he is God's adversary and because he accuses us before God and in our own ears.

In the next chapter, you'll see how Satan opposed Jesus, accused Job before God and accused Joshua and David in their own hearts. Revelation 12:17 describes how he opposes God's obedient children by waging war against them; and Revelation 12:10 reports that he accuses believers before God 'day and night'.

You must have heard a quiet voice telling you that you're no good, that God can't love you, that God won't forgive you, that nobody will listen to you, that nothing will happen, that the vision won't be fulfilled, that you're a terrible sinner, that people would shun you if they knew the truth about you, that you'll never amount to anything much. It's the accuser at work.

Day and night, Satan's forces do his accusing work (as Satan is not omnipresent, you're unlikely ever to hear from him directly yourself). Their aim is simple: they seek to paralyse believers, to con them into inactivity, to neutralise them with self–condemnation, to lull them into a spiritual stupor.

What has the enemy forces said to you? What have they persuaded you not to believe or not to do? For which of their accusing lies have you fallen?

Strip off this mask of accusation and tell them where to go! Believe what God has said to you, and tell the devil that you're going to live by God's words and God's grace – and not by his false accusations.

THE BIBLE OFTEN CALLS Satan 'the tempter', because this is another of his main activities. You already know what this means: by fair means and foul, the devil is constantly seeking to involve men and women in the same alienation from God that he has willingly chosen.

He started tempting humanity in the Garden of Eden, and his forces have been doing it ever since. They don't much care what they tempt you to do, their aim is simply to persuade you to think and act independently of God.

Satan's skill as a tempter is underlined by the frequent biblical descriptions of him as a serpent. This is the mask that he first wore back in Eden when he successfully tempted Adam and Eve to act independently of God's word.

This doesn't mean that Satan is a snake, or that snakes are inherently evil; it's merely that his forces often act in a snake-like way – almost 'hypnotising' their victims into falling under their malign influence.

REVELATION 12:9 MAKES IT PLAIN that Satan, the devil, the serpent and the dragon are different names for one-and-the-same deceiving spiritual creature.

This reference to Satan as a dragon points to his powerful, destructive nature. It suggests that he's a monstrous beast who wreaks havoc and destruction on the earth and seeks to devour men and women.

John's prophetic picture of Satan as a great red dragon, with seven heads, ten horns and seven crowns shows that your enemy is innately destructive, with a multi-form expression, immense but limited power, and widespread authority.

Don't let this prophetic picture frighten you! Although John reports that the dragon makes war against those who keep the commandments of God and have the testimony of Jesus, John also makes it clear that they overcome the dragon by the blood of the Lamb and by the word of their testimony!

In the name of Jesus, you're mightier than the seven-headed red dragon. You don't need to flee from him; if you'll stand firm in the armour of God, you can resist the great dragon and watch him flee.

The destructive, dragon-like, aspect of the devil's character is underlined by the title 'Apollyon', in Revelation 9:11. This means 'the destroyer', and it's why Jesus calls him 'a murderer from the beginning' in John 8:44.

This doesn't mean that Satan is free to kill people indiscriminately: for he can do only what God permits. Instead, it points to the tyranny that Satan's forces exercise over people through the fear of death.

Even so, you should know that demons, especially the Jezebel spirit, are killers by instinct and appetite – with a special taste for God's anointed prophets.

First, they render their captives spiritually dead through trespasses and sins; and, then, they're keen to seal their fate by sickness and physical death – which is part of God's curse on sin.

Death is humanity's last enemy, and the Bible promises that - along with all the other works of the destroyer - it will be finally and fully destroyed by Christ at the last day.

Satan's forces already know what's going to happen. They know that their days are numbered – so they're determined to wreak as much destruction and havoc as they can before then.

But, once again, you've no need to fear. Those people who believe and trust in Jesus have already been set free from the fear of death, because they know that they'll share in Christ's resurrection.

This means that the destroyer's primary weapon should have no effect upon you. It's been reduced to the power of a feather!

Of course, he'll try to convince you that you have everything to fear, but you know that he's bluffing! Laugh in his face and rejoice in your promise of eternal life.

IN EPHESIANS 2:2, the apostle Paul calls Satan 'the prince of the power of the air'. This has nothing to do with geography or meteorology! It was simply Paul's way of explaining Satan's sphere of operations.

Satan began in heaven. He will eventually be banished to the abyss. And, for now, he's between the two. Although he's only a rebellious spirit who has been expelled from heaven, he's still a mighty force with a host of evil accomplices, and has more power than a man or woman.

Satan is a prince with an empire which is staffed by those foul spirits who fell from heaven with him. He controls all the powers of darkness, and pulls the strings of world leaders – political, commercial, sporting and artistic. He rules the darkness of this fallen world, and his chief aim is to keep men and women captive within it.

Paul also refers to Satan as 'Belial' in 2 Corinthians 6:15, and the Gospels sometimes call him Beelzebub. It's hard to know exactly what these mean, but Belial probably means 'spirit of the air', and Beelzebub probably means 'Lord of the dwelling'.

Once Satan's demons get hold of a person, they become the master of the air that the person breathes and the lord of their dwelling.

No matter how much people may mock the idea of Satan's existence, they can't prevent his forces from having a terrible grip on their lives.

Many New Testament passages make the same point. John 12:31; 14:30; 16:11; 2 Corinthians 4:4; Ephesians 6:12 and 1 John 5:19 all show that Satan has a special relationship with this world.

This may be only as a result of his rebellion, but it may also be possible that he was assigned some form of oversight of this world before his fall. He may even have been God's angelic 'Prime Minister' on earth.

Of course, this is only a speculation, but it would account for the very strong links between Satan and our world, and for his vehement hatred of those who delight in re-establishing the kingdom of God on earth.

EVEN THOUGH SATAN IS ONLY A REBEL, the Scriptures make it clear that he is also the spirit behind 'the Antichrist' - the embodiment of opposition to God - that he is the implacable enemy of humanity, and that he is the personification of all evil.

Satan, the adversary, the great accuser of the brethren, is as subtle as a serpent, as violent as a dragon, as deadly as a lion, as deceptive as an angel of light. He is the destroyer, the enemy, the evil one, the real power behind all earthly powers. He is the usurper prince of our world whose rule runs over the whole earth. He is the devil.

The Bible never calls Satan 'the Jezebel spirit', and it's unlikely that the dark spirit behind Queen Jezebel was literally the devil - as he is neither infinite nor omnipresent. Instead, the evil spirit that controlled her is more likely to have been one of Satan's most powerful lieutenants – a terrible principality with the special responsibility of opposing God's prophetic people.

When we read Jezebel's story in the first book of Kings, we can sense this spirit's shadowy form in the background, pulling her strings and guiding her seductive thoughts and violent actions.

You can refer to the devil and his forces by any of the biblical names, for they all point to different aspects of their evil operations. It seems, however, that, at the moment, they are particularly opposed to being identified as 'the Jezebel spirit' – as this exposes the way that they are operating against God's prophetic people today.

If you speak about the evil one, the enemy, the devil, Satan, the prince of the world, evil spirits, principalities, powers, and so on, you won't get much of a reaction. But watch what happens when you start speaking about 'the Jezebel spirit'!

Scores of people will tell you that you should use a different expression, for there's something about this name which seems to be hitting the mark at the moment.

This surely suggests two things. First, that 'the Jezebel spirit' is the satanic being who, under Satan's authority and aided by hordes of howling demons, is currently directing operations against the church.

And, second, that it's trying to repeat the same strategy and actions that it carried out so effectively in the days of Elijah, Ahab and Jezebel.

WHENEVER YOU READ ABOUT THE DEVIL and his forces in the Scriptures, you'll see that they're busy waging war against God's people.

If you are to become a warrior of God who overcomes the Jezebel spirit in your life, your home and your locality, you'll need to know something of their strategies, characteristics and intentions. After all, to be forewarned is to be forearmed!

The single most important fact you must remember is that the forces of evil have no rightful authority over you. Indeed, like Jezebel herself in the days of Elijah, the Jezebel spirit has no rightful authority over any man and woman: it's simply a usurper like its master.

Never give any credence to the devil's false claims to the kingdoms and people of this world – for they rightly belong to Christ.

Satan has been under the judgement of God since the Garden of Eden, and his sentence was executed through the life and death of Jesus. He was dispossessed and bound by Christ, and his power was radically broken.

Jesus bound Satan, and all his forces, by resisting the devil's temptations. He bound him through His gracious healings. He bound him through His mighty acts of deliverance. He bound him by the power of the cross and the resurrection. He bound him by sending the Holy Spirit at Pentecost. He bound him through the ministry of the early church. He bound him through your conversion. And He binds him even tighter every time you obey your Lord and Saviour.

Satan may be powerful, but his power is limited. He has been crippled by Christ. His power has been curbed, his wings have been clipped, his certain doom is in sight, and there is nothing that the devil or any demon can do to thwart God's ultimate plan.

Of course, the Jezebel spirit can still hinder the work of the church, just as Jezebel continually nipped at Elijah's heels – but it cannot prevent the church's ultimate triumph.

It can trick you into silence and apathy, in much the same way as Jezebel's persistent threats tricked Elijah into depression, but it cannot actually stop you from serving God in the power of the Spirit.

Never overestimate the power of devil and his deputies. They are not infinite. They are not eternal. They are not all-knowing. They are not all-powerful. And they cannot be everywhere at the same time. They are merely defeated foes who cannot, and will not, prevail. Hallelujah!

IF SATAN FAILS IN HIS ATTEMPT to persuade you to overestimate his power, he will immediately try to get you to underestimate his power!

Watch out! The Bible makes it clear that, though bound, Satan and his lieutenants are still a dangerous and formidable enemy. Even after God's mighty victory on Mount Carmel, Elijah still had to flee for his life from Jezebel.

You'll have already found that evil spirits have been attacking your mind with doubts and fears and false propaganda. And the more that you love and serve God, the greater these attacks will become – and the greater your strength in Christ to resist them!

You'll have probably found (if you haven't, you soon will!) that demons have been attacking you with lustful thoughts, with self-seeking ambition, with greedy desires for money, position and power, with dislike, hatred, bitterness and crippling unforgiveness.

They attack people with disease, torture, suffering, debt, pollution, poverty and the fear of death. They even infiltrate human institutions - like companies, councils, governments, trade associations, and so on - to wreak havoc and harm.

Daniel 10 describes Satan's mighty princes manipulating nations. 1 Thessalonians 2:18 implies that they control city councils. John 8:44, 59 reveal them influencing rioting mobs. And Mark 4:39 reports that they can affect even the elements of nature.

The Jezebel spirit is a very powerful spirit. Don't underestimate it. You can resist and overcome it in Jesus' mighty name, but it will brush aside any other name with ease and contempt.

Biblical passages like Revelation 12 and Ezekiel 28 underline Satan's terrible violence; the Gospel accounts of demon-possessed people reveal that destructive violence is a common trait; and Matthew 11:12 reports him storming the gates of God's kingdom.

The Jezebel spirit is a violent spirit, and violence is an obvious sign of its presence and activity. Whenever people start to act on the words and promptings of any evil spirit, violence is never very far away.

But the Jezebel spirit is not a mindless thug. It's a highly intelligent being who is crafty, subtle, devious and cunning. Although it's not a creator like God, or as powerful as Satan, it has a fantastic capacity for corruption – and it continually twists and distorts the things of God to cripple the church.

Think of the serpent's skill in tempting Adam and Eve. Consider Jezebel's wheedling advice to Ahab over Naboth's vineyard. Chew on the clever way that the devil attacked Jesus in the wilderness. Then take note of the apostle Paul's words that you need the whole armour of God to withstand the wiles of the devil.

In passages like 2 Corinthians 2:11; 1 Timothy 3:7 and 2 Timothy 2:26, Paul underlines the skill of the devil's forces at catching believers out and gaining an advantage over them.

You have a very clever enemy, who studies you carefully so that it can identify your weakest point and home in upon it ruthlessly. You'll need to equip yourself with every spiritual weapon to resist this evil spirit. And you'll need to depend utterly on the Holy Spirit's anointing and prompting to overcome it.

You've a tough battle ahead. You've a violent and intelligent opponent. But the Stronger One is with you, and in His name you do have the victory.

LIES AND PROPAGANDA are at the heart of the kingdom of darkness. Satan lied in the Garden of Eden when he told Eve that she would not die.

His deputy lied when Jezebel forged documents in her husband's name. And his forces have been lying so much since that Jesus calls the devil, 'the father of lies'.

In many ways, Satan has to be a liar – for his whole strategy of independence from God is built on the lie that sin satisfies when it really leads to death. In fact, everything that the devil and his demons do and say involves some sort of lie which tries to mask this truth.

They lie about themselves, pretending with one breath that they don't exist and with another that they're more powerful than they really are.

They lie about God, pretending that He does not love you, that He cannot love you, that He's got bad plans for you, that He will not forgive you, that His way leads to misery and failure.

And they lie about you, pretending that you're useless, that you'll never amount to anything, that you're destined to fail in everything you attempt for God.

A demon comes to your left ear and whispers a tempting thought, and then dances round to your right ear to condemn you for having such a thought!

As a liar, one of the Jezebel spirit's chief aims is to spread lies in-and-through the church. Just as Jezebel's main mission in life was to promote the worship of Baal in the people of Israel, so one of its chief missions is to spread gossip, false teaching, false priests and false prophets through the people of God.

Passages like Matthew 24:24; 2 Corinthians 11:13; Galatians 2:4 and 2 Peter 2:1 sternly warn you to watch out for false teaching, false believers, false miracles and false leaders.

Be alert for the shadowy, sinister figure behind every person teaching a message which is different from that of Jesus and the New Testament. Your enemy is a very clever liar, so you need to arm yourself with the truth by spending much time studying God's Word.

WE DON'T KNOW whether Queen Jezebel was actually possessed by a demon, but we do know that demons can enter a man or woman. Luke 22:3 and John 13:27 report that this is what happened to Judas.

Evil spirits cannot enter a person without their free will; but persistent, deliberate sin always opens the way for them to enter. For example, the devil gained access to Judas through his love of money and his determination to betray Jesus

Acts 5:3 and 13:10 show that some people can reach the point whereby Satan fills their hearts completely and they become his children. We don't know the extent of Jezebel's control by the Jezebel spirit, but it was plainly the dominant force in her life – and, through her, in the nation at that time.

One of the most striking things about Jezebel was her sheer persistence in opposing the prophet Elijah. She didn't give up when her false prophets were defeated and slaughtered on Mount Carmel; she simply redoubled her efforts to destroy him.

The devil showed the same persistence in his attacks on Jesus. He tried to kill Jesus at birth through King Herod. He tried to kill him through the crowds and priests. And he kept on tempting Jesus right through His ministry, even though Jesus thwarted him at every turn.

Even at Calvary, the devil prompted a man to tempt Jesus to 'save yourself and come down from the cross'.

THE FORCES OF EVIL ARE JUST AS PERSISTENT in their attacks on the people of God. Revelation 12 makes this point very clearly.

First, the dragon tries to devour the man-child when the woman gives birth. When this fails, and the child is caught up to God and His throne, it turns its attention on the woman and her offspring – on the church and individual believers who are faithful to the Lord Jesus.

Be warned, you are facing a life-long struggle with the forces of evil. Every time you resist them, every time you overcome them in one area, they turn round and start tempting and attacking you in another area.

You have most persistent opponents. You just have to be more persistent in resisting them than they are in attacking you. And, in Christ, clothed with the full armour of God, depending on the Spirit's anointing and gifts, you can be.

Remember, on your own you're no match for any demon. They are more cunning than you. They are more intelligent than you. They are more powerful than you. They can deceive you. They can seduce you.

They can enter you. They can ensnare you. They can overcome you. They can murder you.

If you were left to your own resources, you wouldn't have a hope. Thank God that you're not required to rely on your own wisdom and strength! Thank God that you have the victory of Christ. Thank God that He has given you His personal armour to wear. Thank God that He has equipped you with all the spiritual resources you need to overcome your enemy. Now it's up to you to become skilled in using them.

YOU'VE ALREADY LEARNT THAT SATAN was not the only spiritual being to fall from heaven. According to the Scriptures, about one third of the different angelic beings were cast out with him.

Most of the time - in fact, probably all of the time - you will not have any dealings with Satan himself, or even directly with the Jezebel spirit. Instead, they'll send one of their underlings to harass you. Of course, as a pathological liar, this evil spirit will probably pretend that it is Satan just to scare you!

The whole area of the invisible demonic realm is one of the devil's main allies in his war against God.

The Scriptures teach that God is the only source of everything. He made the universe. He made the earth. He made human beings. And He made heavenly beings too. These are generally called 'angels' or 'messengers'.

In Matthew 22:30, Jesus shows that the holy angels will dwell with the redeemed people of God in heaven, and that we will be like them in many respects.

Although 'angel' seems to be the general word for these beings, it's clear that there many different types of heavenly beings.

Jude 9, for example, speaks about the archangel Michael. Genesis 3:24; Exodus 25:20; Psalm 18:10 and Isaiah 6:2 refer to angels, seraphim and cherubim. And Ephesians 1:21; 3:10; Colossians 1:16; 2:10 and 1 Peter 3:22 mention principalities, powers, thrones and authorities.

In the Scriptures, we see angelic beings surrounding the heavenly throne in worship, bringing divine messages of promise and warning to men and women, protecting God's people in times of danger, and appearing at Jesus' birth, resurrection and return.

Jude 1:6 and 2 Peter 2:4 describe how a company of these angelic beings were influenced by Satan to join his rebellion against God. So they fell with him from heaven and shared his judgement.

There are so many of these fallen beings that together they are called 'the kingdom of darkness' and it is their aim to extinguish the light of God and corrupt all the good things that He has made.

For example, Matthew 9:32; 12:22; Luke 9:42 and 13:16 show that these fallen spirits afflict people with illness and suffering – and that Jesus brings perfect healing!

Daniel 10:13–21 and Revelation 2:10–13 reveal that they influence particular places and political regimes.

And 2 Corinthians 11:13–15; 1 Timothy 4:1 and 1 John 4:1 explain that they are deeply involved in deceiving the church and introducing false teaching.

These demonic powers are behind all the destructive forces in our world. They are behind obvious things like the occult, criminal gangs and corrupt political regimes. But they are also deeply involved in the arts, media sports and entertainment world – from where they can spread their anti-God message with great subtlety and guile.

They are also very involved at every level of business - from where they can wreck lives through debt, poverty and greed, ensnare people with 'mammon', and indulge Satan's great love of violent trading.

SATAN IS THE GREAT COUNTERFEITER, and he has forged an evil trinity of allies through whom he aims to establish spiritual independence in people's lives and the church.

This evil trinity comprises 'the world', 'the flesh' and 'the demonic'.

The evil invisible spirits who fell from heaven form the realm of 'the demonic', and it is their mission to bang home the message, 'You will'. You will do this. You will do that. You will not die. You will enjoy this. You will feel good. You will be happy. And so on.

They keep up a constant barrage of propaganda and lies to steer you away from doing 'God's will'.

The devil's second ally, 'the world', is not the planet on which you live. It is the society in which you live, the society that overlooks and ignores God.

We are all greatly tempted and influenced by society. At the smallest level, we feel pressure from the people immediately around us to conform to their way of thinking and acting. We're influenced by our families and workmates, by the programmes we watch and the magazines we read, by our employers and celebrity role models, and so on. Much of this influence is opposed to God's will.

1 John 2:15–17 states: 'Do not love the world or the things in the world. If anyone loves the world, the love of the Father is not in him.

'For all that is in the world - the lust of the flesh, the lust of the eyes, and the pride of life - is not of the Father but is of the world.

'And the world is passing away, and the lust of it; but he who does the will of God abides for ever.'

The apostle John is very strong in his teaching about the world. In 1 John 5:19 he affirms that the world lies in the power of the devil. In 1 John 4:4 he explains that anti–Christian teaching springs from the world. And in 1 John 3:1 he insists that there should be a very clear distinction between the children of God and the children of the world.

John wrote these words almost two thousand years ago, yet they are still strikingly accurate. You live in a society which keeps up a constant message of 'We will'. We will do what we like. We will wear this. We will watch that. We will read this. We will laugh at that. We will sneer at the church. We will buy this. We will mock those who are different. We will gather possessions. We will have no morals. It's anything but 'God's will'.

Do you feel a pressure to conform to the world? Do you feel a pressure to behave like the people around you? Do you feel a pressure to dress in a certain way, to watch particular programmes, to be the same, to spend your money on certain things?

Of course you do! Now you must start to recognise the shadowy sinister figure behind the attractive mask of the world. Ephesians 2:2 says that the devil endeavours to get you to walk according to the course of the world - after all he is the god of this world!

But you can resist. You really can resist the world. Not surprisingly, it is the apostle John who explains how. In 1 John 4:4 and 5:4, he shows that your faith, and the Spirit of the Lord within you, is a far greater force than the world - and that it is strong enough to preserve you from the world's evil pull.

Don't listen to the world's 'we will'. Ignore the pull of fashion. Switch off the advertisements. Don't allow your mind to be polluted by books, films and TV programmes that are blatantly seductive and greed–inspiring. Remember, the world and its 'we will' passes away, but God's will abides for ever.

THE 'FLESH' IS THE THIRD MEMBER of Satan's counterfeit trinity, the third of his allies in his struggle to persuade you to rebel against God's will. The flesh doesn't refer to your physical body; rather, it's a technical term for fallen humanity in its frailty and sin.

In Galatians 5, the apostle Paul teaches that the flesh battles against the Spirit in your life – and you must have felt the titanic struggles that everyone faces between their fleshly desires and God's way of holiness.

The flesh is the seat of your lusts. It's what presses you to satisfy your bodily appetites. It's what drives you towards the misuse of sex, money and power. It's the power behind eating disorders and marital breakdown, behind debt and an obsession with a hobby or sport.

The flesh is a mighty power within you, always pressing you to give in to an evil impulse or wrong desire. It continually whispers, 'I will do this. I will do that. I will wear this. I will reveal that. I will watch this. I will do what I want. I will satisfy myself. I will make myself happy. The flesh never encourages you towards 'God's will'.

The apostle Paul experienced this inner battle, and wrote about his struggle in Romans 7. There can hardly be a believer who cannot identify with his words in verses 18 and 25!

It's Paul, therefore, who explains from his own experience how you can deal with the flesh. In Galatians 5:24, he says that you need to crucify the flesh, to nail those desires down and let them wither away.

And, in Romans 13:4, he urges you to put on the Lord Jesus, to make no provision for gratifying the desires of the flesh.

IT'S ALL ABOUT DISCIPLINE. Some believers seem to think that freedom is simply a question of deliverance. They have a problem with a weakness or a bad habit, so they go forward for prayer and ask the Father to deliver them.

This isn't enough. True freedom involves deliverance and discipline; it involves truth and anointing; it involves revelation and action. The Scriptures do encourage you to pray every day for the Father to deliver you from the evil one; but they also instruct you to nail the flesh dead and to make no provision for gratifying your desires. It's both; not either or.

Deliverance is the easy bit. Discipline is what you do when the deliverance has come. It's what you do when you close this book. It's what you do between meetings. It's what you do when you wake up in the morning with an unhelpful thought in your head. It's what you do when you feel something starting to stir inside you.

It's when you keep on saying, 'God's will be done' rather than, 'My will be done'.

Many people are aware of the devil's strategies, but they have it all in their minds. They read a few books, listen to some sermons, and soon they know everything that there is to know about the subject.

But the truth on its own doesn't bring freedom. For this to happen, the truth must be appropriated, appreciated, internalised, experienced and acted upon under the anointing of God's Holy Spirit.

By the end of this book, you'll know all you need to know about unmasking Satan and overcoming the Jezebel spirit. But this knowledge won't make a scrap of difference unless you take it deep into your spirit, confess it with your mouth, believe it with your heart, and start to put it into practice in your life - everyday.

Remember, even the lowest level of demons know more about Satan than you'll ever know, but they're doomed because they never act on what they know about God's coming judgement. Don't be like them!

AS WE MOVE ON THROUGH THIS BOOK, we'll be concentrating on the way that the Jezebel spirit attacks God's prophetic people, and on how you can overcome it in every area of your life.

Before we do this, though, you need to appreciate that your private struggle with the forces of evil is only one small part of a much bigger war.

You're in a situation of total war, and your opponents are seeking the ruin of everything that God has created.

Satan's number one target is God Himself. Satan wants to dethrone God and replace Him with himself. In his evil ambition and bitter hatred, he has dared to set himself against God.

You can see this in his evil efforts to destroy Jesus – who is Himself God. Satan tried to get Jesus to think and act independently of God's will, to separate the Son from the Father by doubt, disobedience, distrust, disloyalty, compromise and self-seeking ambition. In his devilish attacks on Jesus, he was launching an all-out attack on God. And, in his evil attacks on Christian believers though his demonic underlings, he's trying to break God's heart with the sin and stupidity and ruin of His beloved children.

SATAN'S NUMBER TWO TARGET IS CREATION. He is determined to spoil the whole world and everything that God has made.

The book of Revelation reveals the terrible ways that the enemy attacks our world and all who live here. We see unrestrained war, conquest and military activity. We see civil war and a complete absence of peace.

We see plague and famine, pestilence and malnutrition, pollution and destruction, rampant consumerism and excessive profits.

We see earthquakes, terrors in the sky, demon worship, murder, sorcery, mass persecution of Christian believers, and most people unwilling to repent.

Without the hope of Christ and the certainty of His triumphant coming, Revelation would be a truly terrifying book. The most sobering thought of all, however, is that every description is so true to life. It reads like a TV documentary or newspaper report. It shows how the forces of darkness - they're called Babylon in Revelation - are doing everything that they can to wreck God's world.

CHRISTIAN BELIEVERS ARE THIRD on the devil's hit-list. He's not too bothered with people who are already safely under his control and influence. His major targets are those men and women who have been rescued from his clutches and have committed themselves to his arch-enemy.

This is why your temptations and difficulties increased when you became a believer! You jumped straight into the frontline!

Just as Queen Jezebel sought to eliminate the prophets of God in her day, so the spirit behind her, the Jezebel spirit, seems to be seeking to neutralise the prophetic people of God today.

The book of Revelation contains two important pictures of the way that Satan attacks anointed believers.

First, in chapter 12, there's the image of a bloodthirsty dragon who's waging war against those who keep the commandment of God and bear testimony to Jesus.

If you want a comfortable life, with no opposition, it's easy: just ignore God's commandments, don't testify to Jesus, and the dragon won't bother you!

If, however, you want to be a warrior who obeys God and leads people to Jesus, get ready to feel the dragon's hot breath on your neck.

Second, in chapter 17, there's an image of a seductive prostitute, dressed in purple and scarlet, covered with jewels and gold, holding a cup full of fornication and nameless abominations. She's called Babylon, and she's the image of Jezebel for she's drunk with the blood of the saints and the martyrs of Jesus.

Satan doesn't much care whether you fall for the mask of the dragon destroyer or the mask of the sensuous seducer. The aim of the shadowy, sinister figures behind both masks is the same – it's the neutralisation of individual Christian believers.

WE'RE GOING TO LEAVE ASIDE now the way that the forces of evil grip nations and institutions, encourage involvement in the demonic and counterfeit religion, and seeks to corrupt society and ruin the world.

From now on, we're going to concentrate on the way that the Jezebel spirit directs demonic operations to attack anointed believers - and seek to ruin their ministries, their families and their lives.

You'll learn to recognise its main strategies. You'll grasp how God equips you to deal with these strategies. And you'll see how to take the steps which lead to living in freedom and victory - as a warrior who more-than-overcomes the enemy in every area of your life.

3

Satan on the attack

THE DEVIL HATES GOD'S PROPHETIC PEOPLE, and it seems that he has given one of his most terrible principalities the evil responsibility of orchestrating the forces of darkness against them.

We sense this foul spirit behind the deeds of Queen Jezebel, and call it 'the Jezebel spirit'. This is the evil being who is now intent on trying to prevent you from being effective in your prophetic role in the church and the world.

If you find it hard to understand why Satan hates anointed believers so much, think about it in a slightly different way. An evil spirit is the complete opposite to the Holy Spirit, and is fundamentally opposed to everything about Him.

An evil spirit hates the Holy Spirit with a vicious intensity, and does everything it can to wound, corrupt, spoil and damage His Holiness.

An evil spirit knows that it cannot touch the Holy Spirit Himself, so it focuses its wrath on those people who are in partnership with the Holy Spirit.

It concentrates its attacks on those men and women who are anointed with the Spirit, on those believers who are filled with the Spirit, on those disciples of Jesus whom the Spirit is seeking to use in His power and to shape into His holiness.

If an evil spirit can tempt you to stumble, scare you into silence or seduce you into sinning, it knows that it has pained the Holy Spirit, set back His holy work, and damaged His holy reputation in the world.

This is why the prophet Elijah faced so many devilish attacks. And it's why you must take care to identify how the forces of evil are working in your life – with the aim of neutralising your anointed, prophetic effectiveness and, through your sin, wounding the person of the Holy Spirit.

By now, you should have grasped that the devil is at the root of the evil kingdom of darkness which is trying to destroy all that is of God on this earth. Put simply, he wants to control every aspect of the whole world through his malign forces; and he himself wants to replace God.

Satan's forces dominate the arts. They dominate commerce. They dominate religion. And they dominate politics. They seduce and corrupt men and women in high office, and they capture those in lowly positions.

They wreck marriages, and destroy the lives of innocent people. They are the shadowy, sinister figures behind abortion and infanticide, pornography and seduction, homosexuality and adultery, promiscuity and addiction, gender confusion and rampant greed.

They control all the armies of the world and incite them to war and destruction. They are behind lust, oppression, sickness, racism, consumerism, the fear of death, and every form of exploitation. In short, they are the foul spirits of this present evil age.

IN THE BIBLE, A NAME IS MORE than an identity tag. Names mean something, and they usually reveal something important about the essential calling or nature of the name's bearer.

Elijah, for example, means 'The Lord is (my) God' – and this was the simple message that he was called to proclaim in the power of the Spirit.

Jezebel is another person who had a name to match her nature. Jezebel means 'unhusbanded' or 'without cohabitation' and this is how she lived. She would not dwell with anyone because she had to have control, she would not even be ruled by her husband the king.

Jezebel was the real power in the home, not Ahab her husband. The Queen pulled the strings in the palace, not the King.

She was dominated by an evil spirit who served the one who had tried to usurp God's position and take control of the heavens. So, in turn, she usurped her husband's position and took control of God's nation.

She was controlled by a terrible spirit who fell with the devil because of his fivefold 'I will'; so she was determined to have her own way in all things.

Quite simply, she was 'unhusbanded', she would not be controlled by anyone: she was Jezebel.

This is why many leaders think that 'the Jezebel spirit' is operating in the world again today, for this is exactly how the forces of evil are working at the moment.

Under the authority of Satan, the Jezebel spirit is especially concerned to foster gender confusion among the sexes.

This doesn't only mean homosexuality, for the hairy brute who comes home drunk, beats his wife, and then takes her to bed, is as much under the control of a demon as a homosexual pimp in a red light district.

Rather, the Jezebel spirit promotes a rebellious role reversal of the sexes which urges women to dominate their husbands, to be 'unhusbanded', and which presses men to act like Ahab and let their wives get on with it for the sake of a quiet life.

The Jezebel spirit always fans the flames of its master's original rebellion against God. In particular, it incites the same rebellion against God's order for the sexes that we see in the relationship of Queen Jezebel and King Ahab.

YOU NEED TO GO BACK TO THE BEGINNING to see God's order. Genesis 1:26-28 is Part One of the biblical account of God's creation of humanity. Three phrases in these verses are especially important.

First, God said, 'Let Us make humankind in Our image and let them have dominion.'

Second, the writer comments, ''Male and female He created them'.

And, third, God commanded, 'Be fruitful and multiply, fill the earth and subdue it. Have dominion.'

These phrases tell you that humanity was created in one genus and kind. This can be confusing in those older versions of the Bible which use the word 'man' here. Many centuries ago, 'man' was the common English word for humanity, and the species of humankind was divided into male and female.

Today, of course, 'man' means just men, but this passage is describing the creation of all humanity, not only of men. Male and female were created together by God, and they share a common humanity, a joint dominion and are equal in dignity and worth.

These three phrases also remind you that humanity exists in two distinct forms. This may seem obvious, but it's surprising how confusing it becomes when the Jezebel spirit shows up.

The phrases also make it plain that both male and female members of humanity carry God's image. Remember, God's image was not given only to men!

Although every individual person bears the image of God, men and women reveal God's image in a special way when they come together in a relationship which exhibits the interdependence and order of the persons of God within the Godhead.

The three phrases also show that men and women have an equal part to play in the creation mandate. The divine commandment to have dominion, to be fruitful and to multiply were given to men and women together.

Until men and women in the church end the battle of the sexes, and start to work together in God's intended way, the church will not enjoy dominion, fruitfulness and multiplication in the 'hundredfold' way that God intends.

Christian husbands and wives, believing men and women, you and your spouse, must start to stand together in unity and equality, must begin to work together in partnership – but this can happen only when they follow God's order.

Although men and women equally carry God's image, equally share in human dignity, and are equally called to creation dominion, they cannot fulfil this unless they stay faithful to the order that God has given. You find this in Part Two of the creation story, in Genesis 2.

YOU HAVE TO COMBINE the stories in Genesis 1 and Genesis 2 to get the full picture of creation. For, although both chapters describe the same event, they emphasise quite different matters.

Genesis 2:18 reveals a great deal about men and women. It shows that men and women are essentially incomplete without each other. God made men and women with a fundamental need for companionship, and He made them to meet this need in each other through marriage.

God did not make either women or men with independent spirits, where one needs the other but the other doesn't need the one.

Instead, God made men and women with an equal need for each other, with an equal need for an intimate relationship which enjoys something of the commitment and companionship that exists within the Godhead. This can be properly fulfilled only by Christian marriage.

God designed men and women for marriage, and anything outside this is a perversion of the creation order. Your marriage will start to go wrong when someone or something takes the place of your spouse – no matter whether it is work, ministry, a hobby, children, or another person of either sex. They're all just different forms of adultery. And that is the Jezebel spirit's plan for your life.

GENESIS 2:18 TEACHES THAT THE WOMAN was made to be the man's 'helper' and that the man was made to be the woman's 'head'.

'Helper' is one of the Holy Spirit's names and His main calling, and He's never happier than when He's alongside a believer helping.

So too, in God's creation order, women were designed to be fulfilled when they're alongside their husbands – helping in whatever way is needed.

The Holy Spirit is a submissive helper. He helps you where help is needed and He never pushes you around; and women were made to help their husbands in a similar 'unpushy' way.

If 'helping' is the Spirit's role, 'headship' is Jesus' role, and He revels in providing believers with loving leadership. So too, in God's creation order, men were designed to take the initiative and to provide their wives with a similar, Christ-like, loving leadership.

Of course, demons try to twist this, by encouraging husbands to dominate their wives. But loving headship always consults, always considers, always sacrifices, and always does what is best for the helper.

Did you notice that there is a Holy Spirit role and a Jesus Christ role in the creation order, but not an Almighty God role?

There is perfect order within the Godhead, and the Father, the Son and the Spirit are equal in dignity, worth, beauty and purpose. However, they don't have the same roles and functions.

Though both are also fully God, the Son and the Spirit submit within in the Godhead to the will of the Father. It's the same in God's creation order: the 'helper' and the 'head' are meant to stand together and to obey the will of the Father together.

The first man and the first woman walked in the Garden of Eden with the Father, and every marriage since has been meant to enjoy a similar joint intimacy with the Father.

The 'head' shouldn't order the 'helper' about, saying, 'You will do this and you will do that'. That's not the headship of Jesus. Instead, the 'head' should listen to the Father's voice and gently pass on the Father's will, for it is the Father who is Number One in God's creation order for the sexes.

A few years ago, a famous lady said on public television in Britain that there were three people in her marriage, and the whole world felt sorry for the princess. But every Christian marriage is always meant to involve three people, not two!

Your marriage is meant to be a walk in the garden with the Father - with the husband exercising the loving leadership of Jesus, the wife providing the loving help of the Spirit, and both submitting equally together to the Father.

THE PERFECT HUMAN PARTNERSHIP of headship and helping was soon attacked by the Jezebel spirit.

Genesis 3:6 seems to suggest that the woman sinned first because she took the fruit and ate it, and then gave it to her husband to eat. But the rest of the Bible - for example, Romans 5:12 – shows that God held the man solely responsible. That's what headship involves!

Satan knew that headship belonged to the first man, and he realised that he could corrupt the whole human race if he could strip the man of his headship.

Satan hasn't changed! He's still directing his forces to make the same attack. He's still determined to twist God's order and strip men of their headship. Watch out! Be careful in your marriage that you don't give in to the pressure of the present world to throw away God's good will for your relationship with your spouse.

Satan attacked God's creation order by approaching the woman instead of the man. He started by challenging God's Word and God's character, and then attempted to deceive the woman about the nature of true human happiness.

Satan began by tempting Eve to question God's Word. 'Has God indeed said?' he asked, to introduce an element of uncertainty into Eve's mind about God's will. Satan began by getting Eve to question God's Word, because he knew that there's only a small step from doubting God's Word to disobeying God's will.

The devil's underlings follow a similar pattern today. Be warned! First they lead you to doubt God's Word, then to deny God's Word, next to disbelieve God's Word, and finally to disobey God's Word.

Satan pressed home his attack on Eve by suggesting that she should doubt God's goodness: 'Did God really say that you were not to eat from any of the trees in the garden?'

His inference was that God must be a very mean fellow if He is out to restrict such a legitimate pleasure as tasting fruit from a tree that He'd provided in the first place.

Once Eve was listening to him, Satan started to lie – and told Eve that she wouldn't die. Satan's cunning innuendo was that a loving God would never be so unkind as to punish one of His children. Sadly, billions have gone to hell through falling for the same deception.

Then Satan began to pile on the falsehoods. 'God knows,' he said, that your eyes will be opened on the day you eat, and you will be like gods knowing good and evil in the same way that He does'.

Isn't this familiar! How many times have you heard something similar? 'God's keeping something good from you.' 'You'll like this if you try it.' 'This won't do you any harm.' From Eden to this very day, the forces of evil have kept on presenting things that look good on the outside but which prove to have highly damaging consequences.

Eve fell for it. She saw that the fruit was good for food, pleasant to the eye, and that it would enable her to know good and evil. And, on the day that she ate it, Eve died spiritually. Perfection was ruined. Her life was shattered. And the devil and his demons were delighted.

NEXT IT WAS ADAM'S TURN TO SIN. Genesis 3:6 reports that Eve 'also gave it to her husband who was with her'. What a revealing statement! This suggests that Adam must have been there all along. He'd seen it all happen and had done nothing about it.

God had commanded Adam not to eat the fruit of that tree back in Genesis 2:16-17. He was the head. It was his responsibility to pass on God's will. But he'd watched his wife fall for a deception and had not spoken up by reminding her of God's will.

Do you see how the Satan managed to reverse the gender roles? When he came to the wife, she didn't consult her husband. Instead, she acted independently and usurped his headship. The wife assumed responsibility for the spiritual decision and said 'I will'.

The husband was just as bad, because he stood passively by, not fulfilling his role, relinquishing his headship, and allowing Satan to ruin their marriage.

We don't know how Eve got Adam to eat the fruit, but she probably used one of the new subtle evil devices now at her disposal – persuasion, seduction, manipulation, domination, and so on. It doesn't matter what. She was in charge. She was pulling the strings. She was the head. She told her husband to eat and he did what she said.

Can you see the snake in the background? Has anything been working in your life in a similar way? What are you going to do in the future when you face this particular temptation??

IN HIS HOLY RIGHTEOUSNESS, God had no choice but to punish the sin of Adam and Eve. And this is where the gender problems really begin.

In Genesis 3:16, God told the woman that He would, 'greatly multiply your sorrow and your conception. In pain you shall give birth to children. Your desire shall be for your husband and he shall rule over you.'

Their marriage was perfectly balanced a few verses ago. She was the helper, he was the head., and they walked together with the Father. Now it was all lop-sided. Three things had happened.

First, they were expelled from the Garden and lost their intimacy with the Father.

Second, the woman's desire was now for her husband. This is nothing to do with sexual desire. It's the 'desire' referred to in Genesis 4:7, a desire to dominate and rule. Eve now had a sinful desire to rule her husband, to play God in the home – a desire which she has passed on to all her female descendants.

But, third, the husband now ruled 'over' the woman. He had the opposite desire to his wife – to stop her from ruling, and to hit back and assert himself. The battle of the sexes had truly begun.

After the curse on sin, the woman found herself in a position of weakness and dependence; she resented the man's position and desired it for herself. She sought to gain this by usurping his position and by dominating and manipulating him.

After the curse, the man found that he had been elevated into a position of rulership which was far more dominant than before the fall; and he had a tendency to exercise this 'over' her instead of being a true partner 'alongside' her. Because he was no longer intimate with the Father, he asserted 'his' will instead of passing on the Father's will.

Remember, this is not how God meant it and made it to be. It's the result of sin, and you must not give in to it or accept it. It's simply not good enough to say, 'Well that's how it is.'

You are redeemed in Christ. Because of the cross, the way is open for you to have an intimate relationship with Father. There are no excuses for a believer. You must nail this fleshly desire to rule in the home, and fight this sin as much as you fight every other sin.

Don't allow the Jezebel spirit to wreck your Christian marriage. Don't allow it to twist God's order in your home. If you're single, commit yourself to God's order in the future. If you're a wife, be a Holy Spirit helper. If you're a husband, be a Jesus Christ head.

Stand alongside each other in the mutually interdependent partnership that God has designed. Don't struggle for the dominant position! Bow the knee together to the Father.

IT WASN'T ALL HOPELESS IN EDEN. In the midst of the curse, there is Genesis 3:15. The devil had used the woman to gain a hold on the human race. So God promised to use another woman to bring a second Adam into the world who would destroy his demonic hold for ever. Hallelujah!

You know that God's Genesis 3:15 promise was fulfilled in Christ. He is the Seed of the woman. He crushed the serpent's head on the cross. The rebellious headship of Satan was decisively defeated, and it will be finally and fully destroyed on the last day.

THERE IS A NEW ORDER IN CHRIST, the order of the new creation. You are the redeemed of the Lord, and you must lay down your weapons in the battle of the sexes and go back to God's drawing board.

It's time for you to defeat this strategy of Satan. It's time for you to partner with your spouse according to God's perfect will – so that you can begin to be spiritually fruitful and start to multiply 'one hundredfold'.

It's time for you to rediscover these basic biblical principles, to build on them in your family and relationships, and to defeat the devil and fulfil your dominion calling in Christ.

These days, Satan no longer wears the mask of a primeval serpent. Now he's a shadowy sinister figure who lurks behind the mass media, spreading lies and half-truths, attacking the minds of men and women, fostering a Jezebel-like desire for domination, and ushering people towards ignorance of God's will.

What will you do when a demon next tries to seduce you in this way? Remember, deliverance from this strategy is only by the word of God.

When the tempter lied to Jesus in the wilderness, Jesus used the weapon of God's Word to ward off His opponent. Three times in Matthew 4, Christ said to the devil, 'Scripture says.' If you don't know God's Word, you won't be able to resist him.

Genesis 3:3 shows that Eve actually used this weapon to shrug off the first attack, but Satan is a persistent foe. Eve neglected to use it again, yielded to the temptation, and sinned.

Always be on your guard. Always make time for God's Word. Adam and Eve had no previous experience of such a temptation, and it's when you think that everything is under control that a demon will try to deceive you with a fresh disguise and a devious new trick.

THE STORY OF QUEEN JEZEBEL is a mixture of cunning manipulation and terrible violence. She wheedled, seduced and lied to get her own way; but, if that was not enough, she quickly resorted to bloodthirsty destruction.

Don't think that the Jezebel spirit will attack you only in the same way that the devil attacked Adam and Eve – quietly, deviously, furtively, offering you something which is superficially attractive.

Sometimes he will rampage through your family, attempting to wreak havoc in your lives and trying to leave a trail of suffering behind him in your home – just like Satan did to the man in the Bible called Job.

The Scriptures tell the story of 'a man in the land of Uz called Job' who had to face the devil in the mask of a violent destroyer.

Instead of attacking him with the weapon of lies, Satan came straight at Job with suffering.

And, instead of attacking Job's mind to tempt him to disobey God's will and act independently, he ravaged Job's body in an attempt to make him question God's will, to think independently, and to start feeling acute self-pity.

JOB WAS AN ORDINARY MAN whom God held up to Satan as an example of one of His virtuous servants. Job wasn't a prophet or a priest. He wasn't a judge or a ruler. He was merely an ordinary man who happened to love God.

Don't fall into the trap of thinking that the Jezebel spirit is interested only in 'high-profile' believers. It's opposed to everyone who loves God. It doesn't matter whether you wash the dishes or preach to thousands;

if your heart is for God and His holiness, you're a target of the Jezebel spirit.

God had blessed Job, and he'd become quite prosperous. However, the accuser of the brethren sneered that Job served God and shunned evil only because of the abundance of his material blessings.

So God allowed Satan to test Job to see if he would remain faithful in a time of misfortune and hardship.

First, Satan used two groups of marauding raiders to strip Job of all his animals and servants. Then he used a violent storm to demolish Job's house and kill his ten children.

Faced with all this destruction, Job tore his clothes, shaved his head, fell to the ground, and worshipped God. What would you have done?

According to Job 1:21-22, he said: '"Naked I came from my mother's womb and naked I shall return there. The Lord gave, and the Lord has taken away. Blessed be the name of the Lord." In all this, Job did not sin or charge God with any wrong.'

SATAN WAS FURIOUS when God pointed out Job's continued blamelessness. He insisted that Job's godly attitude and right thinking would change once his own body was affected. So God placed Job in Satan's power – with the sole proviso that Satan must spare his life.

The destroyer went away and immediately attacked Job's body with a revolting and painful sickness. But holy Job was resigned to accepting sorrow as well as happiness from God. When his wife advised him to curse God, Job refused to do so.

Satan didn't inflict the physical suffering as an end in itself. He used it as a means to make Job question God's will, to start asking questions like, 'Why me, God?' 'What have I done?' 'Why aren't you there anymore?' 'Why don't you love me any more?' 'Why aren't you doing something about this?' Does this sound familiar?

After seven days of silence, Job finally cracked and cursed the day that he was born. Chapter 3 records Job's desolate cry of misery and self pity.

When you read the book of Job, and consider the poor advice that he was given by his 'friends' or 'comforters', you'll notice that his friends made a serious mistake.

They assumed that the justice of God must always and automatically reward virtue with blessing, with great wealth and good health, and that any form of suffering must inevitably be the result of sin.

This is still a common mistake. God does bless His people, but the wicked also prosper. And suffering can be the result of sin, but - at times - it is a God-allowed devilish attack.

Think about Elijah after Mount Carmel. What had he done wrong? Under the anointing of the Spirit, he had confronted the false prophets of Baal, called people back to God, seen fire fall from heaven, and executed the judgement of God. There's no sin there!

Did God reward Elijah's faithful ministry with a time of quiet? No, He allowed the Jezebel spirit to come straight at him with the single aim of murder.

If you haven't been through a time of devilish suffering, you will one day. Every believer does. And sometimes this attack of suffering lasts for several years. In fact, we've had to grapple with something like this in my family for over fifteen years, as we've cared for our younger daughter who was damaged at birth by the enemy.

The Jezebel spirit is a particularly violent enemy. It will do everything it can to paralyse your ministry and make you start doubting God's power and questioning His goodness. How are you going to resist it?

IT'S SIMPLE. DELIVERANCE from this particular strategy of the enemy is by the grace of God strengthening your endurance, your faith and your patience. Do you remember learning that you have to persist more than the devil persists? It's the same principle here.

The book of Job is a poetic account of Job's struggle with satanic suffering. Although he was tempted by his wife and his friends to think that he must have caused his own suffering by sinning, Job always maintained his integrity.

Under the unhelpful influence of his 'comforters', Job came close to blaming God and to questioning God's righteousness in His dealings with him. But Job never really denied God's own integrity. Would you fare so well in such circumstances?

When God finally spoke, He did not rebuke Job for his bout of self-pity, and He did not answer Job's questions about fairness and justice; instead, God quietly proclaimed the immensity of His own divine greatness. You can read this in Job 38-42.

By focusing on His divine greatness, power and glory, God was helping Job to take his eyes off his own problems and to see them in a proper perspective – to have a 'cosmic worldview'.

Once Job had begun to concentrate on God again, rather than on himself, he found that his problems and questions had evaporated.

1 PETER 5:8-11 SHOWS that Satan is still out to destroy you through suffering. And verse 10 has been proved true through the ages by countless numbers of Christians. The Jerusalem Bible renders it:

'You will have to suffer only for a little while: the God of all grace who called you to eternal glory in Christ will see that all is well again: He will confirm, strengthen and support you. His power lasts for ever and ever.'

God does not always promise to deliver you immediately from all suffering in this life, but He will be with you in the suffering. He will always hold your hand and give you His strength to help you endure.

Too many believers are provoked by a little bit of devilish suffering into shaking a fist at God and whimpering, 'What have I done to deserve this? I'm your servant, God, I deserve something nice!' 'Why are you doing this to me God? I'd be better off dead!'

Job did not have the benefit of the New Testament. He could not read the apostle Paul's words in Romans 8:18, words which should help you to embrace God's grace and to remain free from the sin of questioning His holy will.

'I consider that the sufferings of this present time are not worthy to be compared with the glory which shall be revealed in us.'

You know how the battle ends. You know who will be finally and fully defeated. You know what will happen to all pain and suffering on the last day. You're on the winning side. All will be well! It's guaranteed in God's Word.

THE NUMBER ONE AIM of every evil spirit is to get you to think or act independently of God's will. It doesn't matter whether you're an ordinary person like Job or a world-famous prophet like Elijah, demons are intent on using every trick in the devil's book to persuade you to join the rebellion – without realising, of course, that this is what you've done!

No demon will do anything so obvious as directly asking you to leave God and join the other side. They're more subtle than that! Instead, they'll try to seduce you with something which is superficially attractive. They'll suggest that this will be enjoyable, pleasurable and harmless. They'll flatter you and insist that you've a right to be happy, that you deserve this comfort, that it's only fair for you to have what you want, and so on.

What no demon will ever do, of course, is suggest that you should check with God first!

And, if you do turn to God's Word for guidance, they're trained quickly to plant doubts in your mind to encourage you to question God's will. They'll ask whether you're sure that this is what God really means. They'll say that this probably doesn't apply to you today! They'll suggest that God won't mind just this once – why, this might even be God's way of blessing you!

Watch out! The forces of evil will tell any lie, send any suffering, fill your mind with any seduction or flattery, to persuade you to think or act 'I will' without reference to 'God's will'.

Resist them, in Jesus' mighty name, and you will see them flee.

THE STORY OF KING DAVID contains two distressing examples of the way that the devil can neutralise the anointed people of God.

David was an ordinary person whom God raised to the highest level of anointed leadership. He owed his position in the nation entirely to God. David wasn't the king because he was the eldest son of a king, he was the king because God had chosen and anointed him. Everything David had was due to God's grace and generosity.

Leaders are not immune to the devil's attacks. In fact, the devil especially targets leaders because he knows the damage that he can inflict on God's people through their fall.

If you're an established leader, never think that temptation is a stage you passed through when you were younger! Temptation is always ahead of you. The devil's forces are persistent opponents who don't give up when you overcome one attack. They merely go away to plan a different one!

If you're a new leader, make sure that you resist the devil's weapon of self-seeking ambition. Squash those thoughts which suggest that you should be more prominent, that the church's ministry would be more effective if you preached a lot more, if you led the worship on special occasions, if you were on the platform every week, and so on.

Remember, the Jezebel spirit is an 'unhusbanded' usurper, and every tendency towards usurping existing leadership comes straight from the pit.

If you're not a leader, recognise that your leaders are particular targets of Satan. Pray for them. Encourage them. Support them. Don't strengthen Satan's weapon of depression by criticising them and running them down – and don't sharpen his weapon of pride by flattering them and boosting their egos.

KING DAVID FELL FOR TWO OF THE OLDEST TRICKS in the devil's book: sex and pride. He caught sight of Bathsheba bathing, and did nothing to resist the fleshly thoughts which filled his mind.

Every church leader knows that adultery is not God's will. No anointed leader starts out in ministry imagining that he or she will ever commit such a terrible sin. Yet experienced, anointed, successful David succumbed to this basic sexual temptation – as, sadly, do some anointed leaders today.

You have a powerful opponent, and the Jezebel spirit is continually using two of the devil's allies - the world and the flesh - to pressurise you into thinking or acting sexually in ways which have nothing to do with God's will. You know that you feel these tempting pressures, but you probably feel too ashamed to admit it.

There are shadowy, sinister figures behind the arts and the media who are promoting the message that God's way of purity is restrictive, repressive, outdated and psychologically damaging, that it's far healthier to be 'liberated', to satisfy your desires, to seek personal fulfilment and happiness, and so on.

They're in league with the shadowy figures who are behind the modern fashion industry and are busily promoting the message that you should dress in a way which is attractive to others – in an alluring manner which turns heads and places distracting, tempting thoughts in other people's minds.

Don't listen to these flattering voices. Don't conform to the world's way of thinking, acting, buying and dressing. Dare to be different; dare to think and act according to your holy God's good will instead of the world's devilish will.

SATAN DIDN'T STOP OPPOSING King David once he'd fallen into sexual sin. After the king had repented and returned to the Lord, Satan came back and attacked him with the weapon of pride.

1 Chronicles 21 tells the story of how the devil incited David to count the people that he ruled and take a census of the Israelites. Despite the objections of David's godly advisor, Joab, this was carried out.

Does it seem to you that this sin isn't nearly as serious as David's adultery with Bathsheba? If it does, it shows that you've been bamboozled by the wiles of the enemy into thinking that there are 'acceptable' sins. God forbid!

Satan had one simple aim: to get David to think or act independently of God's will – to act like a rebel whilst still thinking that he was a godly king!

Satan was as pleased when David was motivated by pride to count his subjects without consulting God, as he was when David was motivated by desire to sleep with one of his subjects.

Both ways, he'd persuaded David to usurp God's will, to think and act 'I will', and so become a rebel. It's sobering to read 1 Chronicles 21 and see the extent of the Lord's anger with the king for acting independently of God's will in this 'acceptable' way.

The truth is that David had nothing to be proud of: the people were the Lord's; the growth of the nation was due to the Lord; the prosperity of the people was due to the Lord; even his position as leader was due to the Lord. His proud thoughts and action were not only sinful, they were also entirely misplaced.

God struck the whole nation because of the pride of its leader. And the devil and his demons rubbed their hands together in glee! Through the pride of the anointed leader, they had managed to damage the whole people of God.

Be careful! You can lead people to the Lord by the dozen, and then be ensnared by the devil into being proud of the dozens. You can manifest powerful spiritual gifts, and then be deceived into being proud of the gifts. In fact, demons almost don't mind if you do overcome them, so long as they can quickly persuade you to be proud of overcoming them! They like that.

How can you deal with the tempting thoughts of pride that demons put into your mind? Deliverance from this snare comes only by unceasing openness to the modest, self-effacing Holy Spirit of God.

Remember, the Holy Spirit never draws attention to Himself; He lives to focus all glory on Another. When you are truly full of the Spirit, and are consciously depending on Him for everything, you will soon recognise that even the smallest smidgen of pride in your life is simply ridiculous.

THAT'S NOT THE END OF THE MATTER. Once you're confidently dealing with the dart of pride by telling the devil that you've nothing to be proud about, it won't be long before you'll hear a demon agreeing with you!

'You're right,' it'll say. 'You really do have nothing to boast about. You're a shocking sinner, look at what you thought yesterday! Why, you're completely unfit to serve God. He'll never be able to use someone like you. Nobody will listen to you when they find out what you're really like.' Does this sound familiar?

This is just another of the devil's old tricks. Zechariah 3 tells the story of Satan's attack on a high priest called Joshua. It shows that the devil tempted this priest to think that he was disqualified from God's service because of his 'dirty clothes'.

Satan attacked Joshua's conscience with tempting thoughts of self-condemnation – in a desperate attempt to lead him into a wrong sense of paralysing guilt at falling short of God's will. Satan didn't mind how he stopped Joshua from exercising his priestly ministry, he just wanted to stop him.

This devilish attack came at a critical time in Jewish history. After forty years of exile in Babylon - a key stronghold of Satan - the Jews had begun to return to Jerusalem.

Joshua's grandfather, Seraiah, had been the High Priest when Jerusalem was captured, and had been executed by Nebuchadnezzar. Joshua's father, Jehozadak, had then been carried off to Babylon as a slave, and Joshua had been born in exile.

It seems likely that some elderly Jews, who remembered the glory of the old days, had suggested to young Joshua that he was unfit to be the high priest because he'd been born a slave in Babylon: they would have said that his time in Babylon had 'defiled' him.

This is what Satan appears to have seized upon when he attacked Joshua with self-condemnation, and is probably what he meant by his devilish gibe about 'dirty clothes'.

How many times have you been attacked in a similar way? How often has an evil spirit suggested that your past somehow disqualifies you from serving God? How frequently have you been reminded of a past failure and a long-forgiven sin? The forces of evil tempt every believer like this – never think that you're the only one!

What will you do when a demon next fills you with a sense of disqualification, defilement, inadequacy and unfitness for the task in hand? Will you still believe it? Or will you have learnt to resist this devilish tactic?

Your opponents are highly intelligent. They don't try to deceive you only with outright lies, they also use a rag-bag of half-truths and false assumptions.

They speak a true statement so that you feel forced to agree with them. Then, having lulled you into a false sense of security, they stab you in the mind with a false conclusion!

In one sense, the accusers of the brethren are 100% right to say that you're a failure, a sinner, and unfit for the task that God has given you.

But they are 100% wrong to say that this means you should fill yourself with self-condemnation and not get on with the task in hand.

The deeper truth is that Christ's blood has delivered you from God's condemnation, and that God's Spirit has equipped you with every resource you need. Nothing else matters.

You can see how God works in Zechariah 3:4-5. An angel said, "'Take away the filthy garments from him'. Then he turned to Joshua and said, 'See I have removed your iniquity from you, and I will clothe you with rich robes.'

God did not disagree with the demonic accusation that Joshua had been defiled. But He did disagree with the demonic conclusion of self-condemnation and uselessness.

The deeper truth was that God had dealt with Joshua's defilement, and was providing the high priest with everything he needed for his priestly service.

Like most believers, you're called to live in the tension between your natural awareness of your faults and your spiritual understanding that you have been fully justified by God.

Satan's forces know that they're onto a winner if they can somehow deaden your knowledge of your justification, or can trick you into thinking that you can somehow lose your salvation.

It's then easy for them to magnify your faults, weaken you with constant reminders about them, and paralyse you with self-condemnation.

Even the most experienced Christian can become utterly condemned by a personal failure or fault. Those demonic whispers, 'God can't use you because...'; 'The reason that nothing is happening is because...'; 'Supposing everyone knew that...' have been heard by millions of believers, and they're still one of the devil's most effective weapons.

Remember, no angel, no prince, nothing that exists, nothing still to come, not any power, or height, or depth, not any created thing, not even the devil himself, can ever come between you and the love of God.

But they can delude you into thinking that you have been separated from God's love. You can then act as if you are separated. And you can conclude that you must be separated. You'll be wrong, of course, but the demons won't mind – they'll be too busy rejoicing at your independent thinking.

THE LITTLE WORD 'IF' is one of the devil's favourite words. 'If God loves you,' a demon says, 'this surely wouldn't have happened'. 'If you were really saved,' it sneers, 'you wouldn't think things like that'. 'If you were genuinely filled with the Spirit,' it lies, 'you'd see many more things happening'.

This little word 'if' should set off alarm bells in your spirit, for it's often a demonic challenge to God's Word and to God's will.

When the devil opposed Jesus in the wilderness, he targeted the fresh awareness of sonship which had come to Jesus at His baptism. The Father had just spoken at the Jordan and announced, 'You are My beloved Son; in You I am well pleased'.

Nothing could be clearer to Jesus. And nothing could be more dangerous to the enemy than for Jesus to know who He was in God.

So the devil launched an immediate attack, 'If you are the Son', he said, 'Do this'. It was a direct challenge to the validity and authority of the voice which had announced Jesus' sonship at the Jordan.

Satan's first temptation then attacked the Son's obedience to this Voice. He pressed Jesus to use His power to meet His personal physical need for bread – rather than to obey the words of the Father to Him.

His second temptation focused on Jesus' desires: the devil offered Jesus fame, acclaim, power and glory, but only if He would worship something, anything, anyone before God.

And his third temptation targeted the Son's trust in what the Father had said to Him at the Jordan. Satan tempted Jesus to prove His sonship – because, he implied, the Voice could not be trusted. He suggested that an experimental leap might provide the proof the Son needed. The demonic implication was that it's not enough to hear the Father speak.

Sons are meant to depend on their fathers – with obedient trust and trusting obedience. So Satan attacked Jesus right at this critical point. Would He rely on the revelation that He had received? Would He depend on the Voice that He had heard? Would He resist the challenge to His knowledge of God's Word? Or would He ignore the Voice and start to think and act independently?

Praise God, Jesus unmasked Satan, exposed the temptations, and refused to think or act on His own initiative. Jesus moved forward into ministry certain that He was the obedient Son who had unhesitatingly believed what the Father had spoken.

What promises has God spoken to you? What vision has He poured into your life? Which direction has He pointed you in? What act of service or ministry has He charged you with fulfilling?

Is His word enough for you about these matters? Are you moving forward in trusting dependence? Or have you listened to the devil's little word 'If' and started to be paralysed?

THE JEZEBEL SPIRIT IS DETERMINED to prise you apart from God, to turn you into a rebellious usurper, to seduce you into wandering into the devil's camp without realising what you are doing. This means that you must constantly guard against giving a demon any access into your life.

Because you have been justified by God, even Satan cannot touch your redeemed spirit. It's simply impossible. You belong to God, and you belong fully to Him for all eternity!

A demon can, however, affect your body through the way that you live in this life. The manner in which you battle against the world and the flesh, and the extent to which you seek God's holiness above everything else, will determine how much access the forces of evil have to your life and family.

The plain fact is that you open your life to every howling demon whenever you participate in the sins of Jezebel and Babylon.

Do you remember learning that freedom involves deliverance and discipline? Christ may set you free from alcoholism, but it's then up to you to stay away from the booze. Christ may deliver you from lustful thoughts, but this doesn't mean that you can now look at certain magazines and things on the Internet with impunity.

The moment that you sin, in thought or in deed, you open the door to the forces of evil and begin to indulge in an activity of the devil. Of course, you're still 'born again'. Your eternal salvation isn't under threat. Christ's blood hasn't suddenly lost its power. But demons can begin to affect your life, to neutralise your spiritual usefulness, and - unless you repent - totally devastate your life.

THE STORY OF BALAAM dramatically underlines this. You can read it in Numbers 22-25.

Balak, the pagan king of Israel's enemy, hired Balaam to curse the nation of Israel so that he could conquer God's people.

But Balaam soon discovered that he was unable to curse them. He told the king, 'Behold, I have received a command to bless, He has blessed and I cannot reverse it. He has not observed iniquity in Jacob nor has He seen wickedness in Israel. The Lord his God is with him, and the shout of a king is among them.'

Every time that Balaam tried to put the devil's curse on God's people, he found that he was speaking words of blessing instead. He could not curse because there was no sin – there was nothing that the devil could grip!

Do you see what this means? If you walk in righteousness, and the shout of the King is heard in your life, every attack of the enemy will become a blessing from God! When you walk in holiness, and listen to the voice of King Jesus, no foul spirit will be able to heap its curses onto your life, your home and your family.

The moment, however, that you stop listening to King Jesus, the second that you start thinking, 'I will live my way', you will provide a handle for the enemy to grip – and it won't be too long before a demon takes hold of you.

Balaam tried unsuccessfully three times to curse Israel. Then he went to the pagan king and gave him some advice which came straight from the Jezebel spirit. In fact, Balaam gave Balak a masterclass in damaging the people of God. This plan was so devilishly perfect, that Satan's forces have been using it against God's people ever since!

Balaam told Balak that cursing wouldn't work while the people of Israel were listening to God's words and obeying them. He advised the pagan king to take one small action – to order some of the loose women in his nation to start to get close to the men of Israel.

Balaam suggested that, after a while, the pagan women should invite the godly men to a party where there'd be some incense burning and some food available which had been sacrificed to an idol.

Then, when everyone was relaxed and the party was going with a swing, the women should start to play a harmless game which involves a little bit of bowing down to Baal – only for fun, of course!

Balaam advised the king to ensure that the pagan women got a bit 'fresh' with the godly men, and then he instructed Balak to sit back and watch the sexual sins which would inevitably start to occur over the following weeks.

Then, Balaam promised, 'the Lord will observe iniquity and will withdraw from His people, and the shout of the king will be silenced among them, and the Lord Himself will rise in fury'.

Revelation 2:14 and Numbers 25:1 show that King Balak followed Balaam's advice to the letter. The people of God set foot in the devil's territory; they ate and bowed to false gods; they committed sexual sins; and the anger of the Lord was aroused against Israel.

In fact, God was so angry that He sent a severe plague which was not stopped until the people of God repented.

This is the only way that the devil can curse those whom God has blessed. The moment that you step out of the protection of Jesus, and start getting involved in one of Jezebel's activities, you provide the enemy with a handle or landing strip.

Because of Christ, you are naturally victorious; but you're in deep trouble when you give a demon an entrance into your life.

Because of Christ, you have real power over sin, and your standing before God is unalterable; but any demon can treat you like an unbeliever when you continue in sin.

You'll still go to heaven - nothing can ever change that - but you'll be plagued with hellish misery here on earth. And you'll also miss out on your eternal reward in heaven.

THE DEVIL IS DETERMINED to get you to sin, for this means that his demons can then start to wreak havoc with your life. They're not bothered what sin you commit, any sin will do, so long as you start to think or act independently from God.

Eve usurped her husband's role as head, then doubted and disobeyed God's word. Adam ducked his God-given responsibility, staying quiet when he should have acted, and obeying his wife rather than his God.

Job cracked under the weight of suffering and started to question the character of God. He cursed the day that he was born and shook his fist at God, almost blaming Him for his misfortune.

David didn't resist the dart of desire, and ended up in bed with another man's wife. Then he didn't resist the arrow of pride, and ended up proudly numbering 'his' subjects and achievements.

The king should have known better. He should have trampled on his fleshly desires. But Satan somehow managed to deceive him into providing a toehold, which soon grew into a foothold, which soon became a huge landing strip, and you know the rest of the story.

Joshua heard two voices. One said that he was to serve as God's High Priest in Jerusalem; the other told him that he was unfit for the job, that he was a slave who'd spent too long in Babylon, that he didn't match up to his father and grandfather.

So which voice did Joshua believe? The wrong one, of course – that's why he was paralysed by a sense of self condemnation and uselessness? Thank God that he listened to God in the end.

It was much the same for Elijah. The mighty prophet of the Lord experienced victory after victory, but he still ended up sitting under a tree wishing that he were dead, thinking that he was the only believer left in the land, deeply depressed and scared out of his skin.

If you go through the Bible with a toothcomb, you'll find only one person who persistently and consistently always overcame the enemy. Only one man who never gave the devil the tiniest toehold. Only one person who resisted every attack, trampled on every temptation, and never thought or acted on His own initiative.

Suffering never made Jesus blame God. Taunts about the circumstances of His birth never silenced Him. Threats of violence never put Him off. Rejection and betrayal by His friends and family did not plunge Him into depression. Quite simply, Jesus is the triumphant overcomer.

He is the One who is with you and within you. You're not being directed by somebody who fell and failed, by someone like Eve or Elijah, David or Job, Joshua or Balaam; you're being guided by Jesus the more-than-a-conqueror.

If you listen only to Him, you're certain to be kept safe. If you do only what He says, you're bound to know God's blessing. If you go only where He sends, you're sure to live in the security of God's will. If you speak only what He prompts, you're guaranteed to know the quiet authority of God. If you think only His thoughts, the mind of Christ will be in you and you will prove what is the good and acceptable and perfect will of God.

Of course, Jesus will lead you along the way of the cross, and the Jezebel spirit will urge its demons to throw everything at you, but nothing will be able to harm you.

Stay close to Jesus. Listen to the voice of the King. Depend entirely on His strength and ability. When you live with deliverance and discipline, you'll be able to trample on the tempting thoughts of sex and pride, to swipe away the darts of doubt and depression, and to ignore the meaningless attractions of money and power. In short, you will be a true warrior of God.

4

Jezebel exposed

THE MALIGN FORCE THAT FELL FROM HEAVEN, that is implacably opposed to God and His prophetic people, is a dangerous masked bandit who operates in many different ways.

You can call him Satan or the devil. You can call him the tempter, the accuser or the destroyer. You can call him the prince of darkness or the spirit of this evil age. You can call him Babylon, Belial or Beelzebub. He is all of these and worse.

But the one name that his evil forces seem to hate hearing more than the rest is 'the Jezebel spirit'. For this draws attention to a moment in Bible history which exposes how they are operating today. When you use this name, you unmask the demonic strategy at work in the days when Queen Jezebel waged war on the prophet Elijah.

Most people are more comfortable speaking about 'the spirit of the world' than 'the Jezebel spirit'. This is because the Jezebel spirit cannot abide being named – for the name strips off its mask and reveals exactly what it is like.

According to 1 Kings 16, Ahab was a particularly wicked king of Israel. He continued the sins of King Jeroboam and carried on trying to mix worshipping the Lord with worshipping local pagan deities and nature.

King Ahab also allowed the city of Jericho to be rebuilt, in direct disobedience of God's Word, and married Jezebel 'the unhusbanded', the woman 'without cohabitation', a princess of Tyre who promoted the false religion of Baal to God's people.

Within a few years, Jezebel had usurped the role of her husband and become the real power in the land. She personally financed over 800 false prophets and actively advocated the worship of the false gods Baal and Ashteroth throughout Israel.

Behind the queen's evil activities, there lurked the evil spirit that is always determined to corrupt and pollute God's people. 1 Kings 18 describes how the prophet Elijah was raised by God to destroy the work of this spirit in his day. Verses 36-49 report the dramatic confrontation on Mount Carmel.

'It came to pass, at the time of the offering of the evening sacrifice, that Elijah the prophet came near and said: "Lord God of Abraham, Isaac and Israel, let it be known this day that You are God in Israel and I am Your servant, and that I have done all these things at Your word."

'"Hear me, Oh Lord, hear me that this people may know that You are the Lord God and that You have turned their hearts back to You again."

'Then the fire of the Lord fell and consumed the burnt sacrifice and the wood and the stones and the dust, and it licked up the water that was in the trench.

'Now when all the people saw it they fell on their faces and they said, "The Lord He is God, the Lord He is God". And Elijah said to them, "Seize the prophets of Baal, do not let one of them escape".

'So they seized them and Elijah brought them to the brook Kishon and executed them there.'

Do you see what happened? The fire came when the hearts of God's people turned back to the living God. If you turn to God with real biblical repentance, and forsake sin so fully that no demon can get even the tiniest toehold in your life, the fire of God will fall on you in a similarly spectacular way. You won't know what's hit you!

YOU'VE ALREADY SEEN that Elijah's name was his ministry. He was Mr TheLordismyGod and this was what he was called to announce.

After the fire, when the people cried, 'The Lord is God', they were not only declaring the Lordship of God, they were also acknowledging Elijah's ministry.

Elijah was not just a run-of-the-mill prophet, he was specially anointed by God to confront and defeat the Jezebel spirit in his own generation.

Many years later, God raised a second Elijah - John the Baptist - who ministered in the power and spirit of Elijah to confront the forces of darkness and prepare the way for the first coming of the Lord. John the Baptist ministered in a day when another evil king ruled Israel, and this time the Jezebel spirit had the prophet's head on a platter.

Today, at another critical moment in history, when evil rulers abound on the earth, God is beginning to prepare the way for the second coming of the Lord.

This time, God is not seeking to raise a single Elijah figure to confront the Jezebel spirit in one limited location. Rather, He is seeking to raise a whole prophetic Elijah generation who will defeat the whole force of this spirit wherever it is operating in the earth.

God wants to establish a complete generation of Spirit-filled men and women who do not fear Jezebel, who have been transformed to the extent that their very natures declare 'The Lord is my God'.

God longs for you to be part of this end-time Elijah company. He wants you to be His anointed Elijah in your home, your church, your workplace, your locality.

He is commissioning and equipping you to call men and women to repent, to summon people back to God, to confront the enemy forces, to overcome the Jezebel spirit, to see the fire of God fall through your life and your ministry.

As the second coming of the Lord draws nearer, so it seems that the Jezebel spirit is becoming ever-more frantic in its devilish work of orchestrating demonic opposition to God's prophetic people.

This evil spirit is approaching its final manifestation - just as the Kingdom of God is moving towards its fulfilment - and God is preparing an Elijah people to confront it: a people with the message 'the Lord is my God' on their lips, in their hearts, and running through every aspect of their lives.

AFTER HIS MIGHTY VICTORY on Mount Carmel, Elijah allowed himself to become intimidated by Jezebel's threats.

The anointed man who had opened and closed the heavens, who had called down fire from heaven, fled before the words of a woman.

Jezebel's words were not idle threats, as Elijah knew that she'd already massacred hundreds of God's true prophets. She really meant to kill Elijah, because she was in the grip of the violent spirit who hates God's prophetic people.

The higher that you go in the Spirit like Elijah, the more that you'll have to face this level of spiritual opposition. Many believers are not prepared for the great intensity of the spiritual battle, for the sheer ferocity of the foul spirits who hate God's prophetic people.

They raise their heads above the trenches, aim a few pot-shots across No Man's Land towards the enemy, and then start to crumble when their finances are hit, their marriage comes under pressure, their children are assaulted, and they are rejected and criticised.

'It's not worth it Lord', they whimper, even though they can hear the Holy Spirit urging them on, promising them deliverance when they break through to the other side.

Remember, it's total warfare. If you want to be an effective warrior of God, you've got to learn to ignore the fear and intimidation of the enemy and to press on regardless with the task that God has given you.

When you do concentrate on God and His love - rather than on the devil and his threats - you'll soon experience the truth of the promise that God's perfect love casts out all fear.

JEZEBEL WASN'T OPPOSED ONLY TO ELIJAH, she was an active persecutor of all God's prophets. She was out to destroy anyone and everyone who'd been anointed with the Spirit by Almighty God. 1 Kings 18 describes how small groups of godly prophets had to hide in caves to escape her demonic persecution.

Throughout history, the demonic spirit behind Jezebel has repeatedly persecuted God's people as in the day of Elijah. There's hardly a nation on earth which hasn't been influenced by this foul being at some stage in its history to restrict, oppose, imprison, torture and kill those who follow Christ.

Even though the church in Britain is not suffering in this way at the moment, there is more violent persecution around the world today than at any other time in history.

The devil's pea-shooters of mockery, materialism, doubt, seduction and self-seeking ambition have paralysed large sections of the British church for several generations, so the Jezebel spirit hasn't needed to resort to the devil's exocet of persecution for almost two hundred years.

All this will change, however, when we rise up as a holy prophetic people, engage the enemy forces, and preach the message of salvation and repentance.

Revelation 17 reveals the extent of the persecution that God's people will have to face in the end-times: it will be so extreme that 'the woman' will be 'drunk with the blood of the saints and with the blood of the martyrs of Jesus'. It's a sobering passage.

You need to settle your attitude now, before the enemy forces become active again in this way in your location. Decide now, whether you live or die, that Jesus will get the victory.

If you live, promise to live to do damage to the devil. And, if you die, promise to die with a testimony which destroys him as you go to be with Jesus. Remember, for you to live is Christ, but to die is gain.

THE BIBLE SHOWS THAT QUEEN JEZEBEL was a very manipulative and controlling woman. Don't make the mistake, however, of thinking that Jezebel was manipulative just because she was a woman! She only behaved like this because she was controlled by the Jezebel spirit.

This spirit manifests itself as much through men as through women, and the church contains an equal share of controlling men and manipulative women – both groups are under the direct influence of this evil spirit.

In fact, Ahab was as much under its influence as Jezebel. He yielded to his wife's manipulation and gave up the headship of his home and his nation to this pagan princess.

1 Kings 21 describes how Ahab wanted Naboth's vineyard for himself. He looked out of his bedroom window, and said something like, 'That would make a nice vegetable garden for me, too bad it's somebody else's vineyard. I know, I'll go down there and negotiate with the owner. I'm sure that he's a decent chap and will sell it for a reasonable sum'.

So Ahab visited Naboth and told him that he would like to buy his vineyard. But Naboth refused to sell, saying: 'No you can't, it's my inheritance. You're not taking my inheritance away from me'.

The immature king stormed home, went to bed, refused to eat, and sulked because he couldn't get his own way.

Once the queen had found out why her husband was sulking, she told him that she'd show him how to be a real king - and soon had hatched a plot.

She said, 'Get people to accuse Naboth falsely, then kill him at a feast, then take the vineyard for yourself'. It was a typical scheme straight from the depths of the pit, for it involved lies, violence and a covetous lust of possessions.

The plan was quickly carried out. Naboth was slandered then killed. Jezebel gave Ahab the vineyard.

And the Word of the Lord came to the prophet Elijah. Interestingly, God didn't send the prophet to rebuke Jezebel, He sent him instead to confront Ahab and blamed him for this wicked deed.

God said, 'You shall speak to him, Ahab. Thus says the Lord "Have you murdered, have you also taken possession?" And you shall speak to him saying "Thus says the Lord, in the place where dogs lick the blood of Naboth, dogs shall lick your blood."'

Why did Ahab get the blame? It was because he'd yielded to his wife's manipulation. It's the Adam and Eve principle over again. Although the wife was the main manipulator, the husband was held responsible because he'd not carried out his headship responsibilities.

WATCH OUT! Demons are after your inheritance too. They want to steal everything from you that is rightly yours in Christ. They'll offer you anything you want - sex, money, power; you name it, they'll promise it - if you'll relinquish your spiritual inheritance.

Stand firm. Don't be swayed by its offer. You have a pearl without price. There's nothing it can offer which compares to the love and grace and blessings of God.

Then, when you've stood firm, prepare yourself for violence – for you'll have aroused the rage of a terrible spirit.

Beware, too, of controlling people in the church. When you're feeling low and disappointed, perhaps even sulking a little, watch out for that smotherly person who comes with false comfort and manipulative suggestions.

This foul spirit controls too many congregations through 'manipulative mothering'. You know what this is, you've seen it in your church. Just because the words are gentle and the smile wide, it doesn't mean that a servant of the Jezebel spirit isn't in the background behind the motherly mask.

THE TRAGEDY IS THAT NONE of this would have happened if Ahab had carried out his creation role. If he'd been the real head of his household, Queen Jezebel would have been kept in line. But the king abdicated his creation responsibility and handed over his position and authority to his wife.

Right from the Garden of Eden to today, the Jezebel spirit has been encouraging men to run away from headship, and has been pressing women to usurp headship.

Men abdicate their headship either by giving up and saying, 'You make all the decisions, it's your business', or by becoming so aggressive and forceful that they act like a tyrannical dictator rather than a loving leader.

The Jezebel spirit doesn't mind whether a man is a wimp or a tyrant, for both are equally damaging. It does mind, however, when a husband exercises the loving, gentle, sacrificial leadership of Christ, and when a wife helps with the love and care and skill of the Holy Spirit.

It hates godly marriages and Christian families, and is determined to smash your marriage with whatever weapon is to hand. Together with your spouse, guard your headship and helping roles. Bow the knee together to the Father and walk in a threesome with Him. In the name of Christ, resist the enemy's attacks on your marriage, and see this spirit flee.

THE BIBLE RECORDS THAT AHAB and Jezebel lived in great affluence and luxury. They didn't care about the poor in the land and they ignored the poor on their doorstep. In fact, they exploited the poor for their own selfish advantage.

Revelation 17 shows that the end-time force of darkness, Babylon, is characterised by the same affluent luxury, love of money and callous exploitation of the poor. Revelation 17:4 says that, 'The woman was arrayed in purple and scarlet and adorned with gold and precious stones and pearls, having in her hand a golden cup full of abominations and the filthinesses of her fornication'.

And Revelation 18:3 notes, 'For all the nations have drunk of the wine of the wrath of her fornication. The kings of the earth have committed fornication with her, and the merchants of the earth have become rich through the abundance of her luxury.'

Whether you realise it or not, you're under tremendous pressure from the world, that evil ally of the devil, to love money, to seek wealth, to acquire possessions, to trample on the poor overseas and prosper at their expense, to ignore the poor in your land, and so on.

Sadly, the pressure of the world to serve 'mammon' is so great that some preachers have started to use the biblical teaching about prosperity as a cover for their personal greed.

You live in a consumerist society which worships the false god 'mammon' with the same fervour and devotion that Jezebel worshipped Baal. Its false prophets use the propaganda of advertising and the subtle pressures of the media to encourage thinking and actions which are at loggerheads with God's Word.

Jesus' clear teaching about money is mocked, ignored or distorted. The Bible's instructions about tithing and free-will offerings are either held up to ridicule by the world or selfishly abused by some parts of the church. The idea that debts should be freely forgiven is lampooned as utopian nonsense.

Can you see the shadowy, sinister figure behind all this? Do you recognise Jezebel's manipulative voice, urging you on toward 'more for myself'? Can you see her fingerprints on multi-national companies, the international media and some Christian ministries?

Watch out! Babylon is being built in your day right under your nose. Jezebel is hatching her greedy plots all around you. Stand firm against them. Have nothing to do with the selfish, consumerist greed of 'mammon'. Heed the words of Jesus that nobody can serve two masters, that it's a straight choice between God and Money.

Demons will whisper in your ear that this word doesn't apply to you. It's a lie. You're as vulnerable to the desire for Naboth's vineyard as the next man or woman, and you need to stand firm against it at all times.

ALTHOUGH THE OLD TESTAMENT doesn't offer a specific example of Jezebel's sexual immorality, the New Testament insists that she was a seductive woman.

The whole area of seduction, sensuality, immorality and perversion are more of the chief weapons of this Jezebel spirit, and they're all a sickening perversion of the good thing that God has made.

This spirit doesn't aim to smash Christian marriages only through twisting the headship and helping roles, it also aims to destroy them through seduction and a wrong use of human sexuality.

Don't think that demons are only at work in this way on late night television and Page Three of some newspapers. They're also active in churches and Bible Colleges too.

This is how it works. Here's a nice young man of God with a destiny and a vision, so along comes a seduction of Satan. A woman sets her eyes on this young man – and, years later, after the seduction is over, she discovers that he's not the great man of God she thought when she mimicked him in the prayer meetings. And he finds, too, that she's not the beautiful, submissive, eyelid flashing, very carefully positioned near him, lady that he thought she was!

It happens the other way round as well. The young man isn't so irritable when the lady is around. He prays just that little bit longer and louder. He catches her eye when he's preaching. He asks her to help him pray with him for a needy person, then suggests that they all link hands while they're praying. You've seen it!

Many men and women in our churches and fellowships have never repented of this spirit of seduction. You can tell this by the way that they dress. They're the men in tight trousers who've clearly spent more time in front of the mirror than on their knees before God. And they're the women who carefully leave a small gap between the garment on their top and the garment on their bottom!

It's the Jezebel spirit of seduction! Repent of it. Change the way that you dress. If you want revival, you may have to change your wardrobe, and you'll almost certainly have to do something about what you watch on television.

Don't beat about the bush. You know that much of what appears on television is deliberately seductive and arousing – it's the Jezebel greed show at 8.00, the Jezebel glamour show at 10.00 and the Jezebel girly show at 11.00.

Why do you watch? What's it doing to your mind and your spirit? Why are you allowing demons to fill your mind with seductive, unsettling, disturbing thoughts? You're playing with fire.

You don't need a set of legalistic rules to live by. You don't need to throw away all the paraphernalia of modern living. You just need to use some spiritual common sense. What is the point of subjecting yourself to unnecessary temptation? It's just plain stupid.

Do you know what Jezebel did when King Jehu came to destroy her? 2 Kings 9 reports that, as soon as she heard about his mission, she put paint on her eyes and adorned her head and looked through a window! What was she doing? She hoped that a little bit of seduction would distract Jehu from his act of judgement.

It's not the make-up and the after-shave that's wrong in itself, it's the way that you use them. In the same way, things like films, music, television and clothes are not wrong in themselves, it's the way that they're used and the way that you allow them to affect you.

Of course God wants you to make the most of the looks that He's given you. But he doesn't want you to use your looks, or your clothes, or your words and gestures, to attract a man or woman by seduction.

If you get your man or your woman through some form of seduction, you're inviting the Jezebel spirit to control your marriage from then onwards. Repent of this now. Deal with it, and God will set you free.

2 KINGS 9:22 STATES that Jezebel was involved with witchcraft, and Revelation 18:23 insists that sorcery is part of the end-time business community.

The moment that you yield even to the slightest of these evil manifestations, you're submitting to the power of witchcraft.

Just as the devil isn't a cartoon character with horns and a tail, so witchcraft and sorcery aren't about broomsticks and magic spells. They're far more dangerous than that!

The merchants of our world are trying to place you under a spell. They are trying to make you behave in the way that they want. They are trying to make you buy what they want you to buy. They are trying to make you wear what they want you to wear. They are trying to make you think and act in the ways that they want you to think and act.

Quite simply, they're trying to control you. They call it marketing and the profit motive. The Bible calls it sorcery and witchcraft.

Look at the billboards around you. Listen to the adverts on the television. Can you see that it's the same old spirit of deception and seduction that was at work in the day of Elijah – opposing the people of God and trying to hold the whole world captive.

Can you see how the devil's forces use seductive, deceptive controlling images in the world of media, sport and the arts? They don't care what people worship, what controls their lives, so long as it isn't God.

They don't care whether people worship Manchester United or the Spice Girls, spend all their money on Nike products or Nintendos – it's all the same to them. Just so long as people are controlled by something other than God.

These seductive spirits are very active in the world of the arts, and any believer who works in this area must make sure that they've dealt with the spirit in their own life.

It's the same in the world of business and commerce. This world is controlled by the evil spirit 'mammon', so you'd better make sure that there's no mammon spirit in you before you enter this area of life.

Remember what the devil said to Jesus, 'You can have all of this so long as You serve me'. Will he promise anything less to you? Of course not.

If you're to be a triumphant overcomer, there must be no compromise, no compromise at all with the forces of darkness.

THE NATION OF ISRAEL worshipped the true God, the living God who made heaven and earth, the all-loving, all-powerful, all-healing, all-knowing Yahweh. Jezebel worshipped the false god Baal, and she did her utmost to persuade the people of God to worship Baal too.

You must be very careful at this point. It's easy to think that the devil is primarily concerned to keep unbelievers captive through religions like Buddhism, Islam and Hinduism. This is part of his mission, but he is even more eager to seduce and deceive God's people into worshipping false Gods.

Remember, the Jezebel spirit hates God's prophetic people, and seeks to involve them in the worship of something like Baal. It wants to get a foothold in the modern church so that some form of false religion can pollute and paralyse God's people.

This spirit's troops work in obvious ways like doubt and compromise, and also in less obvious ways like legalism and fleshly exhibitionism.

They try to get some of God's people to worship a particular leader, rather than God alone. They try to get another group of believers to emphasise one narrow facet of God's truth to excess, rather than holding the whole of God's word in balance.

They try to fan the flames of schism and disunity, for they know that this does more to paralyse the mission of the church than anything else. They aim to get one group to worship a particular version of the Scriptures, another to be exclusively committed to their own congregation, and another to start criticising and denouncing just about everyone else.

It's all different forms of deadly false religion, and the Jezebel spirit is determined to establish it in your church – through you.

Resist this foul spirit. Worship God, not man. Listen to the whole counsel of God, not one small section. Maintain the unity of the Holy Spirit. And encourage the believers and congregations around you with frequent words of commendation.

THE JEZEBEL SPIRIT IS A REBEL AND A USURPER just like its master. It fell from heaven as part of the original rebellion against the authority of God, and is implacably opposed to God's Word and God's will.

You can see this in the Garden of Eden, when the devil tempted Adam and Eve to reject God's Word and go their own way.

You can see this in the life of Queen Jezebel, who was compltetely opposed to the prophets who proclaimed God's Word.

You can see it in Satan's violent opposition of Jesus, who is Himself the Word of God.

And you see it in Revelation 17, where the beast on which the 'woman' is seated is full of names of blasphemy – which is the antithesis of God's Word.

All demons are dead against God's Word. They are the sinister, shadowy figures behind the endless sniping at God's Word on the media.

They are the foul forces that tell you to read something else, to broaden your horizons, to feel too embarrassed to read your Bible on the train, to doubt and question and disbelieve and disobey what God has written for your good.

Resist them. Treasure God's written Word. Read it regularly. Read it fully. Rely on it completely. Value God's spoken Word. Be zealous for prophecy. Pay attention to God's teachers. Test everything that you hear, but obey what you know God has said.

The Jezebel spirit will always want you to rebel against God's Word. Don't do it. Instead, get to know God's Word so well that - like Jesus in the wilderness - you can use it to defeat the devil's underlings whenever they attack you.

1 KINGS 22 REPORTS THAT AHAZIAH, the son of Ahab and Jezebel, 'walked in the way of his father and in the

way of his mother. Sadly, he was as influenced by the Jezebel spirit as his parents had been before him.

Like all spirits, the Jezebel spirit is a hereditary spirit. These spirits pass from one generation to another until they are stopped by the power of Christ through renunciation and repentance.

After Ahab died, Ahaziah became king and carried on doing evil in the sight of the Lord. It was hereditary; but there was an element of hope, because the son didn't go as far as his parents had done.

This shows that evil spirits can be pushed back, that they can be broken and they can be defeated. Hallelujah!

Like Ahaziah, you may be under pressure because your parents or grandparents were deeply influenced by a demon. However, there's no need to despair. In Christ, its power can be broken in your life. There is deliverance. You can be free, and you can make certain that your children are free too.

THERE IS MUCH IN THE WORLD today that speaks of the Jezebel spirit.

It is the shadowy sinister figure behind infanticide, abortion and euthanasia. It's behind the mask of life-dominating problems like gambling, debt, alcoholism and drug abuse.

It's behind greed, covetousness and consumerism. It's behind anger, rage, jealousy, pride and self-seeking ambition. It's behind bitterness, unforgiveness, adultery and marital breakdown.

It's behind every form of opposition to the church of God, and every form of opposition to prophecy and the anointing of God.

Don't compromise anything. There are no grey areas in the Bible and the Christian life. It's either right or it's wrong. It's either of God or the devil. The whole of your life, from now to eternity, should involve a struggle to discover God's will in a situation.

Demons will surround you with voices that suggest 'I will' or 'we will' or 'you will'. Your duty is simply to listen intently to God and establish 'His will' - and then to do that - without any compromise.

The demons will be furious, but you'll be safe in the centre of God's will. There's no better place to be!

5

the way of victory

THE BOOK OF REVELATION GUARANTEES that a great day is coming when the forces of evil will be finally and fully destroyed. It promises that the day is drawing ever nearer when the foul spirit that opposes God's prophetic people, that manipulates and controls every aspect of our society, is going to fall.

Revelation calls this spirit 'Babylon', and describes how it controls the world and persecutes what is of God in the world. Then it promises that God will move swiftly in judgement through angelic intervention, and that Babylon will fall in a single hour.

What does this promise mean for you? It means that all God's judgements are righteous and true. There is no escaping them. They are real. They will happen. If God says judgement is coming, it's coming.

God's judgement is going to fall on Babylon, and on all who side with Babylon and Jezebel. Although every believer will escape the eternal fires of hell by faith in Jesus Christ, some believers will be subject to this judgement – but only those who have sided in some way with the works of Babylon.

God is speaking to you now prophetically, through Revelation 18:4, about Babylon: 'Come out of her, my people, lest you share in her sins, and lest you receive of her plagues.'

You probably know that I believe the Bible teaches, 'once saved, always saved'. Make sure, however, that you don't understand this to mean, 'once saved, then live as you like'!

Instead of offering you a license to sin, God's Word instructs, 'once saved, fear the name of the Lord'; 'once saved, the power of sin is broken in your life'; 'once saved, turn away from your sin and embrace Jesus Christ'; 'once saved, lay hold of your spiritual inheritance'; 'once saved, come out of the world's way of thinking and living'.

The redeemed people of God are supposed to stay out of the Jezebel life of sin and rebellion. They're not meant to drift back into it a few years after their conversion! If they do, they're participating in the sins of Babylon, and the Revelation plagues of divine judgement will come on them. That's the stern word of the Lord.

God is beseeching you to have nothing to do with Jezebel's way of living. He's urging you onward to holiness in your life. He's pleading with you to come out of Babylon and to turn away from your sin – for this is the way to freedom and victory.

THE BOOK OF REVELATION REMINDS YOU that there is a deeper reality than the world you can see with your physical eyes.

The world is not rolling on endlessly in a chaotic fashion; there are spiritual forces at work behind everything that you see, and everything is moving inexorably towards a titanic conclusion.

The closer you come to the return of Jesus Christ, the greater will be the manifestation of both the Jezebel spirit and the Elijah anointing.

As you seek to move in the Elijah anointing, so you will have to learn how to confront the Jezebel spirit. After the fire on Mount Carmel, Elijah fled because he didn't know how to overcome the fear and intimidation of Jezebel. He had to be led by the Lord back to Horeb, back to covenant mountain, to learn how to fight.

God gave him an assistant, Elisha, and a fresh vision. Then, between their two anointed ministries, Jezebel was finally destroyed in that generation.

God's purpose for your generation is the same as back then. As Christ's return draws nearer, so God is pouring more of His power upon the body of Christ and spreading His ministry among more believers.

God's purpose today is to prepare an entire generation of Elijahs and Elishas who will minister together to turn the hearts of the fathers to their children, and the hearts of the children to their fathers.

This will be a generation which sees marriages restored under the power of the end-time Elijah anointing; a generation which hears the voice of the Lord echoing from shore to shore in ever-increasing cycles of revival and renewal; a generation which watches waves of repentance sweep the nations as God prepares the way for the coming of the Lord.

At the same time, however, this generation of modern-day Elijahs and Elishas will also see an uglier face of end-time revelation.

It will stare with horror as Satan's kingdom begins to flourish. It will watch with apprehension as the wheat and the tares grow side by side and thrive in the same environment. It will gaze with shock at an ever-increasing manifestation of the Jezebel spirit, even to the extent of the Babylon spirit in Revelation 17-18.

And the great cry of the Holy Ghost to this prophetic generation is, 'Come out of her, my people, lest you share in her sins, and lest you receive of her plagues.'

Go all the way with God! When you smell Jezebel a hundred yards away, go a hundred miles in the other direction so that you have nothing to do with the kingdom of Satan.

Be totally committed to Christ, without even a tiny hint of anything that speaks about this satanic kingdom. You've been born free, so be free. The slavery of your old existence to Satan has gone, so live free from Satan. You've been set free from the power of darkness, so don't dwell in darkness.

The deep spiritual reality is that the power of Satan has no hold over God's redeemed people. You have been set free from Satan, and from all hereditary bondages.

1 Peter 1:18-19 states: '...knowing that you were not redeemed with corruptible things, like silver or gold, from your aimless conduct received by tradition from your fathers, but with the precious blood of Christ, as of a lamb without blemish and without spot.'

You've been redeemed from the empty way of life that was handed down to you from your forefathers. You've been redeemed from their religious traditions, from their ideas and culture, from their unhelpful philosophies and negative habits.

You've been set free; you've been redeemed by the blood of the Lamb!

Because of Christ's victory on the cross, the truth is that you share in His victory over Satan. You have authority over the devil and his demons – in Jesus' precious name. You have victory over sin, death and the grave. You even share in His victory over every opponent of the gospel.

This is how you began the Christian life. You began in a place of total victory, and you should have gone on from there to become more-than-a-conqueror.

The deepest truth is that you have Christ's victory on the cross as your birthright. When you were born into the kingdom of God, you were born completely free.

When you were saved, you were set free from the power of the devil. You were set free from the power of darkness. You were set free from every evil thought. This is your birthright.

Even if you've slipped back since then, nothing can change the fact that this is your birthright. Right now, as you read this page, you can pick up your birthright and start to live in the good of it. Nothing can prevent you from doing this! Nothing!

THERE'S MORE! Along with this birthright of victory, God has also given you some very effective weapons of spiritual war.

He's not given you these powerful weapons to put on the wall and admire. He's given you these weapons so that you can take His victory and enforce it; so that you can exercise dominion over the invisible realm.

You've learnt much in this book about the weapons and strategies of the enemy. They are cruel weapons and evil strategies, but they're like dust and ashes compared to the weapons and wisdom that God has given to you.

You have the effective weapon of prayer with which you're called to wrestle with Satan and his accomplices. This isn't long-distance, push-button warfare; it's face-to-face grappling and groaning.

The devil has no greater aim than to stop you from praying, to sever your communication link with your Commander-in-Chief. But you have the belt of truth to protect you from lies like, 'God won't hear you'. You have the breastplate of righteousness to save you from giving up when the enemy whispers 'You can't pray, remember what you thought yesterday'.

And you have the army boots of eager readiness to spread the gospel, with which to stamp on temptations not to bother to pray for guidance or boldness: 'Do it tomorrow', the demons always say.

You have a huge shield of faith, almost the size of your front door, soaked in living water to extinguish every fiery dart of doubt: 'This won't work. There'll be no change. You're wasting your time.' And you have the crash helmet of safety to help you keep praying when a stunning blow falls – illness, accident, redundancy, bereavement, and so on.

These mighty weapons do not place you in a war-free zone – they enable you to survive and to conquer in a violent holocaust. The devil's knockout blow will give you a headache instead of a broken skull! Read Psalm 124 and get the matter in focus.

If a demon cannot stop you from praying, it will try to distract you with temptations. Use the sword of the Word of God to fight off the temptations of ambition and grandeur - as Christ did in the wilderness. This sword is the rhema of God: it's not limited to the Bible; it can include a spoken word or a prophetic utterance.

Having done this and stood firm, you're to pray at all times in the Spirit. Satan-defeating intercession isn't an occasional prayer, it's a costly wrestling that involves: '...praying always with all prayer and supplication in the Spirit, being watchful to this end with all perseverance and supplication for all the saints.'

YOU'VE ALSO BEEN EQUIPPED with the mighty name of Jesus. When you speak His name, every invisible knee must bow. Every knee! Every demon! Every time!

You can't overcome the enemy in your own name, through your own strength, or because of your own experience. As Revelation 12:11 states, you overcome, 'by the blood of the Lamb and by the word of their testimony, and they did not love their lives to the death.' Don't forget the last part of this verse!

Jesus said, 'Don't be frightened of the one who can kill the body, I tell you somebody you should fear. Fear the one who can destroy both body and soul in hell.'

You should have a living, awesome, loving fear of God, but you shouldn't fear the forces of the devil. If you are willing to die for Jesus, there's absolutely nothing that the devil can do to you. But if you fear for your life, he'll soon have you in bondage.

IT DOESN'T STOP THERE. The Scriptures also promise that the anointing of the Holy Spirit will destroy the yoke of bondage. If you've been anointed with God's Spirit, your anointing is another weapon you can use against the forces of evil.

In Mark 11:23, Jesus reveals the extent of the authority that you have in Him. 'Whoever says to this mountain, "Be removed and be cast into the sea," and does not doubt in his heart, but believes that those things he says will come to pass, he will have whatever he says.'

Don't neglect to put this into practice.

Praise is part of your armoury too. In Matthew 21:16, Jesus quotes from Psalm 8:2, 'Out of the mouth of babes and nursing infants you have ordained strength, because of Your enemies, that You may silence the enemy and the avenger.'

Then Matthew 18:18 shows that whatever you bind on earth - if you're doing it under the direction of the Holy Spirit - will be bound in heaven, and that whatever you loose on earth will be loosed in heaven.

This is serious stuff. The Scriptures aren't exaggerating. They aren't trying to push you into a vulnerable position where you'll be smashed by the enemy. On the contrary, they're cataloguing the powerful weapons that you've been given and showing you how to use them.

Do you believe God's Word? Are you ready to use your weapons? Are you going to be a warrior or a wimp? It's surely time now for you to join the Elijah company and to prepare for active service

IF FREEDOM AND VICTORY ARE THE BIRTHRIGHT of all redeemed believers, why aren't all believers living in victory and freedom? What's the problem?

Sadly, very few believers know who they are in Christ. Because the devil is terrified of what will happen when you know exactly who you are in Jesus, he does his utmost to keep the truth from you. Large numbers of believers spend much of their Christian lives being bound by things from which they were set free at spiritual birth. It's tragic!

There's a famous old painting of a believer. He's looking from a prison cell at night, holding on to the bars, and his eyes show that he yearns to be free.

Behind him the cell door is wide open; but the prisoner doesn't know this. All he has to do is turn around and walk through the open door – but he stays in the prison clutching the bars. It's a powerful, prophetic painting of many in the church today.

Of course, by now, you know that the door is open and that the devil has no power over you. You know that you're free, and you're determined to live in victory.

Don't forget, however, that the moment you yield any part of your life to sin, you put yourself back into bondage. As free as you are in your position in Christ, when you entertain unrepented sin in your life you build a landing strip for a howling demon to come and attach itself to that part of your life.

While it is utterly impossible to conceive of your eternal liberty in Christ ever being completely broken by the devil, you must recognise that you give a temporary toehold to a demon when you engage in any of the activities of Jezebel.

The moment that you get involved in greed, violence, love of money, sexual sin, unclean thoughts, pride, rejection of the Word of God, manipulation, worship of false things, and so on, you open a door to a demon.

It only needs a tiny toehold, then - if you don't repent - it'll work this into a foothold, then into a kneehold, and eventually into a stronghold. It really is this simple.

AS YOU'VE READ THIS BOOK, you'll have come to realise that you're not living as God wants you to live. You're not being as fruitful as He intends, you're not multiplying 'one hundredfold', and you're not resisting the Jezebel spirit in every area of your life.

God has been speaking to you while you've been reading. He's been pointing out those things that need to put right, those things you need to stop thinking and doing, those things you need to start believing and acting upon.

It's time now for you to move forward, to pick up your birthright, to take fresh steps along the path of freedom and victory.

THE FIRST STEP IS FOR YOU TO CONFESS YOUR SIN like David confessed his sin with Bathsheba. He said to God, 'Against you, you only have I sinned, and done this evil in your sight – that you may be found just when you speak, and blameless when you judge.'

Confession involves a wholehearted abandonment of sin. When you sin, you sin wholeheartedly. When you confess your sin, you abandon it completely.

All you want is to be right with God, nothing else matters. You want to get away from your sin because you're ashamed of it and embarrassed by it. You want to get out of the devil's activities. You want to snap off his handle on your life. You want no more fellowship with the unfruitful works of darkness. You don't want to participate in the plagues of Babylon. In short, you want to get the heaven out of there!

Confess your sins! Do it now. It doesn't matter if you're reading this on the bus or the train. It's more important to get right with God than to make a good impression on someone you may never see again!

CONFESSION IS GOOD BUT IT ISN'T ENOUGH. It's only the first step on the path of freedom, not the first and the last step.

When you confess, you're agreeing with God's holy attitude to your sin. You're aligning yourself with His way of thinking. You're saying the same thing that God says about your sin. You're owning your sin; now you must disown your sin.

Pay attention to Isaiah 55:7. 'Let the wicked forsake his way, and the unrighteous man his thoughts; let him return to the Lord, and He will have mercy on him; and to our God for He will abundantly pardon.'

Can you see that this is not just going forward at a meeting, confessing your sins, and then going back to your seat still carrying your sins?

Forsaking your sins means leaving your sins at the foot of the cross and walking on with Jesus without them.

Forsaking your sins means returning to the Lord. You can't bring your sins with you when you come to the Lord. You have to release your sins because holy Jesus is there. You have to throw away the whole way that you live - seven days a week, at work, rest and play.

NEXT, YOU MUST FORGIVE all those who have sinned against you. This is what Jesus taught in Matthew 6:14-15:

'If you forgive men their trespasses, your heavenly Father will also forgive you. But if you do not forgive men their trespasses, neither will your Father forgive your trespasses.'

In this verse, Jesus isn't talking about the 'judicial' forgiveness you receive in the final court where God is the judge of all humanity. He isn't talking about standing before God as judge. Instead, He's talking about your relationship with your Father whenever there's sin in your life.

When there's a problem in a family, the parents have to sort it out. When their child sins against them - as they do - the parents need to deal with the matter. But they don't say, 'Because you've sinned against us, we won't be your parents anymore.' That's ridiculous!

Jesus isn't talking about you losing your salvation. He's talking about your heavenly Father. Like any earthly parent, God will hold your sin against you until you put the matter right. It will sour the relationship, but it won't sever it!

Jesus explains that you get right before your Father by forgiving other people. Quite simply, if you want to come and receive parental forgiveness from your heavenly Father, and are withholding forgiveness from somebody else, you are exposing yourself to demons.

If you don't believe this, read Matthew 18:34-35: 'His master was angry, and delivered him to the torturers until he should pay all that was due to him. So my heavenly Father also will do to you if each of you, from his heart, does not forgive his brother his trespasses.'

Who are the torturers? They have to be demons, which means that unforgiveness exposes you to demonic torture. Be warned! Nothing demonises a person more quickly, more permanently, more severely than unforgiveness. It's just not worth it. Obey Jesus instead. Forgive those who've sinned against you. Do it now.

YOUR NEXT STEP along the pathway of freedom is to ask God for deep cleansing and forgiveness.

When David came in confession to God, Psalm 51:7 reports that he said, 'Purge me with hyssop, and I shall be clean; wash me, and I shall be whiter than snow.'

If you've ever done any washing, you'll know that there's a big difference between washing and purging. Some things you can wash, but other things you just have to purge.

Sin goes so deep, is so hard to remove, and leaves such a dark stain, that it needs the radical surgery of purging.

When the prophet Isaiah took the living coal onto his lips, God announced, 'Your sin is purged, your iniquity is atoned for'. Purging isn't a symbolic washing of sin, it's the burning away of the entire nature associated with sin. It's a total transformation so that holiness of life can begin.

Ask God to purge you now. Ask Him to impart the nature of Christ's pure righteousness and holiness into your life. Commit yourself to walking in your newly purged state, in perfect cleanliness and total holiness.

THEN YOU MUST EXPEL every evil presence in your life. The Christian life is a relationship between God and you.

There are some things that only God can do, and there are other things that He expects you to do.

One of the devil's favourite devices is to get you to try and do what only God can do, and to get you to keep asking God to do what you should be doing yourself.

For example, a demon will press you to try to purge yourself of sin through will-power and self-discipline, and then it'll get you to ask God to resist the devil for you!

James 4:7 sets out your responsibilities: 'Therefore submit to God. Resist the devil and he will flee from you.'

You don't need someone else to pray for you; instead, you need to submit yourself to God. You don't need God to deal with the devil and his demons - He did that at Calvary - you need to resist them yourself.

Resist them now. Resist the devil. Resist the Jezebel spirit. Resist the forces of mammon and Babylon. Resist the world, the flesh and the demonic. Use your weapons. In Jesus' mighty name, expel every evil presence in your life. Don't beat about the bush any more. Start behaving like an Elijah warrior.

FINALLY, YOU MUST SEEK A FRESH INFILLING of the Holy Spirit. You must ask God to fill all the areas which have been purged and cleansed, all the parts of your life where evil has been expelled.

When I was seeking God, just after He had spoken to me about the Jezebel spirit, I received a fresh infilling in my life in two particular areas. There had been no room for God before, because two demons had been binding me in the core of my being. They were to do with things that Jezebel had implanted in an effort to destroy my life.

Then, after God had wonderfully delivered me, there was ample space for a fresh filling and anointing with God's Spirit. It's the same for you. God does not want to leave you empty. He wants to fill you with Himself, to saturate you in His Spirit, to anoint you with His grace and power.

This is the beginning of freedom, the first steps of victory, your first strides along the path of liberty. Now that you are free, it's your duty to stay free.

THE WORLD THINKS THAT FREEDOM means doing what you want, how you want, when you want, where you want. God calls this bondage to the rebellious Jezebel spirit. True freedom is knowing God's will, doing God's will, thinking God's will, going God's way and living God's will. It's total dependence on the Lord; it's yielding constantly to Him.

Freedom isn't only something that God does at the beginning of your Christian life, it's also a lifestyle that you must continually maintain. Galatians 5:1 says: 'Stand fast therefore in the liberty by which Christ has made us free, and do not be entangled again with a yoke of bondage.'

YOU LIVE IN FREEDOM by standing fast in Christ's achievement, by not budging one inch from the cross. You stay in freedom by following Christ to the cross, and then by pursuing God with all your heart – wherever He may lead you.

You can be sure of at least one thing when you are pursuing God – that you're travelling in the right direction!

If you are pursuing God, it follows that you must be fleeing immorality, fleeing youthful lusts, fleeing greed, fleeing all the devil's activities.

So, if you want to live in freedom and victory, run to Jesus. If you want to see Satan unmasked, run to Jesus. If you want to overcome the Jezebel spirit in your life, your home and your family, run to Jesus.

What is there for you to play around with in the world? Why are you wasting time on things that don't matter? Seek God. Pursue Him. Everything else pales into insignificance and piffling irrelevance compared to His beauty and love.

Some people seem to think that holiness involves legalism – if it did, however, it wouldn't be holiness. Pursuing God isn't legalism. It's a delight. It's a pleasure. It's the greatest joy in the world.

We don't pursue Him because we're cowed in spirit and are acting in fear and reluctance. No, we're like the psalmist who says:

'One thing I have desired of the Lord, that will I seek: that I may dwell in the house of the lord all the days of my life, to behold the beauty of the Lord, and to inquire in His temple.'

'As the deer pants for the water brooks, so pants my soul for You, O God. My soul thirsts for God, for the living God. When shall I come and appear before God?'

PRAYER, AS A FAMOUS POET WROTE, is the Christian's native breath. It should be as natural for you to pray as it is for you to breathe – and you should pray with every breath that you take.

Some people asked Smith Wigglesworth, a great Apostle of Faith in the first half of the twentieth century, about prayer. They said, 'Smith Wigglesworth, you're a man of faith and miracles, you've raised umpteen people from the dead. You've cast out more demons than we've had hot dinners. Tell us, how long do you pray everyday?'

'Well,' the apostle replied, 'I don't ever pray any longer than twenty minutes'.

'What?' his questioners exclaimed. After pausing for effect, Smith Wigglesworth continued, 'Yes, but I never go twenty minutes without praying'.

The apostle was trying to say that prayer is not something which can be measured in minutes. Prayer is a lifestyle. Prayer is constant two-way communication with God. Prayer is essential to living in freedom.

GOD WILL SPEAK TO YOU through prayer, and He will also speak to you through His written Word. Just as prayer should be more than a twice-a-day habit, so reading God's Word should involve more than a few verses last thing at night and first thing in the morning.

In John 8:31, Jesus doesn't call you to read a few notes to set you up for the day; He says: 'If you abide in My word, you are My disciples'.

Don't just read the Word, abide in the Word. Don't just skim through your favourite passages, study the whole of God's Word fully. Live in the Word and let it dwell in you richly.

Through actively listening to God and reading His Word, you'll soon come to know His will and His ways. You'll get to know God's attitudes and desires. You'll understand what He expects you to think and to do in most situations.

Then comes the crunch. Are you going to be one of those believers who knows everything about God and His will in their minds, or one of those who actually does His will in their lives?

James 1:22 urges you to: 'Be doers of the Word, and not hearers only, deceiving yourselves'. Head knowledge of God's will is not enough. Walk in active obedience to the Lord. Allow His Word to direct and control your thoughts and actions. Go only where He sends. Say only what He prompts. Do only what he commands.

There can be no presumption and no disobedience on the path of freedom. It's all 'His will' and no 'I will'.

THE WAY OF FREEDOM IS LIFE AND JOY. It's a delight not a chore. It's grace not law. Those who walk this way soon start to develop a lifestyle of worship, praise and thanksgiving. Not only is this a natural response to freedom, it also has a negative effect on demons. They can't come within ten miles of a praising saint, for the sound gives them a headache!

Some people become far too serious and introspective about the faith. They are so worried about doing the wrong thing, that they don't ever do the right thing! They are so cautious that they become idle, and the devil soon finds work for idle hands!

You don't need a direct Word from the Lord to guide you about which pair of shoes to wear. You don't need to pray for guidance before choosing from the menu in Mcdonalds. And you don't need special direction to do those things that have already been made clear in the Scriptures.

It's always right to maintain good works and active service. Don't stay at home moaning and moping and waiting for a special revelation, get out there and serve soup to some tramp on the street who needs Jesus.

Visit an elderly person who lives on their own and is craving for contact with somebody younger. Fetch their shopping. Mow their grass. Cook them a meal. Invite someone round who needs cheering up. Do something good! Get in the habit of doing those things that you know please God!

PURSUING GOD ON THE PATH OF FREEDOM is not a solitary activity. It's something you should do with others, not on your own.

It's one thing to keep a clear conscience before God, but another thing to have a good conscience before people. They tend to get upset by little things that don't bother God – and they're not so quick to forgive you!

It's hard, but you have to work at your relationships with other believers – as nothing attracts people to Jesus more quickly than healthy relationships, and nothing repels them faster than disunity and squabbling between brothers and sisters.

You need to work at this at several levels. It doesn't just involve being on nodding first-name terms with the people in your congregation. You also need to work at establishing a positive relationship with every believer in your locality – not just those in your tradition or denomination.

More importantly you need to be an active part of a small group of believers, of a cell. If you're not part of a small group like this, you are exposing yourself to danger and failure.

In church meetings and services, you are 'fed' from the front, but in cell groups you're fed from every side. In church services, there's no opportunity to ask any questions; in a cell you can interrupt and ask how this point applies in your situation.

People get to know you a little in a congregation, but they get to know you really well in a cell. They know your worries and problems, they share your joys and triumphs, they help you to overcome your weaknesses and shortcomings. Cells are a vital part of staying on the path of freedom.

YOU'VE JUST ABOUT REACHED THE END of this book now, and it's time for you to decide what course of action you're going to follow.

Are you going to join the Elijah company of men and women who are determined to overcome the Jezebel spirit in every area of your life and locality?

Are you going to resist every dart of the enemy, every doubt and temptation, every desire and ambition, every independent thought and deed?

Are you going to claim your birthright and live in the freedom and victory that Christ accomplished for you with His shed blood at Calvary?

Are you going to live with radical holiness, pursuing God, running from every sin of the enemy, living in the light before other men and women?

Are you going to forsake sin, embrace purity, and be a warrior of God who does good in the world and damage to the devil?

Come before God now and vow to turn away from everything that is displeasing to Him. Refocus your heart, your life, your all on Him. Dedicate yourself afresh to walking in repentance and joy.

Affirm that Jesus is Lord over your spirit, your soul and you body. Declare that no other spirit is ever going to Lord it over you again.

Announce that you will not be subject to any spirit other than the Holy Spirit, that you will fight every evil spirit, that you will never serve a false god.

There is only one God and only one way to God, and His name is Jesus.

God is calling you closer to Himself than ever before. Run to Him now, join His Elijah generation, and stay with Him forever.

6

confess and forsake

As you've read this book, God will have spoken to you about some things in your life which have displeased Him and given a demon a toehold. You know what they are.

If you want to overcome the Jezebel spirit in your life, you must be willing to forsake all your sin, and to live a life of holiness and righteousness before God.

Look at the sample list on the next few pages, and add anything to it that the Holy Spirit shows you. Use it to guide your confession.

When you confess your sin to the Lord, make sure that you are very specific. If, for example, pride is one of your problems, don't just say, 'Lord, forgive my pride'. Tell Him how you have been proud. Confess the specific areas of pride in your life. Admit what, exactly, your proud attitudes are. Mention specific people and situation when you tend to commit this sin in thought or deed.

These sins aren't in a particular order, and it's unlikely that you will need to deal with all of them. You need the Holy Spirit to show you what needs to be confessed and forsaken, and to highlight those areas that are particularly important.

pride

self righteousness

abdicating headship

usurping headship

greed

self-seeking ambition

love of pleasure

love of money

meanness

sinful entertainment

immoral thoughts

pornography

occult involvement

fornication

adultery

homosexuality

seductive behaviour

compromise

questionable pursuits

unforgiveness

judgementalism

criticism

anger

hatred

resentment

lovelessness

not showing mercy

not caring for the poor

not practising hospitality

dependency

independence

controlling habits

drug and alcohol abuse

idolatry

lying

breaking your word

unbelief

doubt

cynicism

self pity

prayerlessness

disunity

envy

covetousness

not honouring your parents

self condemnation

fear

impatience

intolerance

presumption

disobedience

a prayer for deliverance

Father, I come to You and confess my sin in Your presence.

(Name and confess every sin that the Holy Spirit has revealed to you.)

I renounce, reject and forsake my sin in Jesus' name.

I forgive all those who have sinned against me.

(Name those who have hurt you.)

I release them now, and ask You to bless them richly in Jesus' name.

I take authority now, in Jesus' name, over every activity of Satan in my life. I reject and renounce every spirit of 'Jezebel' and 'Babylon', every evil, troubling, controlling and seducing spirit. I command every spirit that has gained access to my life to leave me now. I loose myself from every demonic bondage and influence over my life, my family and my body.

Father, I now ask you to fill me with Your Holy Spirit. Touch my life with Your love, and send me out to live for You and to serve Your people, now and forever. Amen.

a declaration of deliverance

I confess and declare that I know and enjoy the absolute freedom of God. Jesus Christ has set me free from the guilt and power of sin. I am free indeed.

I have been crucified with Christ, and have been raised into His resurrection life of perfect liberty.

I know that the Son of God was manifested with the purpose of destroying all the evil works of the enemy. And I know that He has done this in me.

I walk in the freedom of the Spirit, and have been liberated by the law of love. I have been delivered from the curse of the law, and I am no longer bound by sin the flesh, the world or the devil.

I announce that I am now free to do right, to obey God's will, and to serve my Lord and Saviour with every part of my being.

I know that I am not my own, for I was bought by a great and blood-stained price. I now belong to Jesus, and am eager to do His bidding. I renounce sin, Satan, and all his evil selfish works. I stand firm in my freedom, and live in the victory of Christ forever.

If you want to share your personal testimony about overcoming the Jezebel spirit, or would like to request prayer, or would like some information about Kensington Temple and the London City Church network, please write to:

Kensington Temple/London City Church
Kensington Park Road
London
W11 3BY
England

If you would like information about other helpful books, tapes and videos, please contact:

Dovewell Mail Order
Kensington Temple
Kensington Park Road
London
W11 3BY
England

Tel: 0800 521631
Fax: 020 7729 7343